WILDLIFE
AND
PLANTS

Third Edition

Volume 8

Marshall Cavendish

Marshall Cavendish Corporation
99 White Plains Road
Tarrytown, New York 10591-9001

www.marshallcavendish.us

Library of Congress Cataloging-in-Publication Data

Wildlife and plants – 3rd ed.
    p.   cm.
    Rev. ed. of: Wildlife and plants of the world. c1999.
    contents: v. 1. Aardvark – baboon – v. 2. Bacteria – bladderwort – v. 3. Bluebird – chickadee – v. 4. Chimpanzee – crane fly – v. 5. Cricket – earwig – v. 6. Echidna – flying fox – v. 7. Flying lemur – grass – v. 8. Grasshopper – horseshoe bat– v. 9. Horseshoe crab – ladybug – v. 10. Lamprey – maple – v. 11. Marlin – muskrat – v. 12. Mustard -- oxpecker – v. 13. Palm – polar bear – v. 14. Polar regions - raven – v. 15. Ray – sea lion – v. 16. Sea urchin – sponge – v. 17. Spore-bearing plants -- termite – v. 18. Tern – warbler – v. 19. Warthog – zebra – v. 20. Index.
    ISBN-13: 978-0-7614-7693-1 (set : alk. paper)
    ISBN-10: 0-7614-7693-8 (set : alk. paper)
    1. Animals – Juvenile literature. 2. Plants – Juvenile literature. I. Wildlife and plants of the world.
    QL49.W539 2006
    578 – dc22   2005058219
    ISBN-13: 978-0-7614-7693-1 (set : alk. paper)
    ISBN-10: 0-7614-7693-8 (set : alk. paper)
    ISBN-13: 978-0-7614-7701-3 (v. 8 : alk. paper)
    ISBN-10: 0-7614-7701-2 (v. 8 : alk. paper)
Printed in: Malaysia
11 10 09 08 07 06   6 5 4 3 2 1

Marshall Cavendish Corporation

Project editor: Marian Armstrong
Editorial director: Paul Bernabeo
Production manager: Michael Esposito

The Brown Reference Group plc

Editorial consultants:
• Mark Hostetler, Ph.D., Department of Wildlife Ecology and Conservation, University of Florida
• Joshua Ginsberg, Ph.D. • Jefferey Kaufmann, Ph.D.
• Paul Sieswerda, Ph.D., Wildlife Conservation Society
• Special thanks to the Department of Botany, The Natural History Museum, U.K.

Editors: Anne Hildyard, Wendy Horobin, Selina Wood
Picture researchers: Brenda Clynch, Laila Torsun
Illustrators: Bill Botten, John Francis, Peter Bull
Designer: Sarah Williams, Lynne Ross
Managing editor: Bridget Giles

Picture credits

Front Cover clockwise from top left: John Foxx Images; Photodisc; Photos.com; Photodisc; Digital Stock; John Foxx Images; Photos.com; Photodisc; Digital Stock; Photos.com; Digital Stock; Digital Stock.

Back Cover: John Foxx Images

FLPA: Hoskings, David 508; Withers, Martin B. 509; **NHPA:** Ausloos, Henry 460, 505; Balharry, R. 472; Bannister, Anthony 455, 486, 493; Blossom, Joe B. 506; Buckingham, John 484; Cambridge, G.J. 480; Campbell, Laurie 481, 494; Carmichael, James H. Jr 458, 487; Currey, Dave 504; Dalton, Stephen 454, 483, 485, 495, 500; Danegger, Manfred 502; Dennis, Nigel J. 496, 497; Erwin, Robert J. 475; Goodman, Jeff 490; Ingen, Hellio & Van 503; Janes, E.A. 464; Kirchner, Rich 474; Krasemann, Stephen 459, 473; Leach, Michael 470, 471; Moosrainer, Gonter 456; Papazian, Ashod 461; Paton, William, S. 466; Planck, Rod 462; Robinson, Steve 492; Shaw, John 463, 488, 489; Strange, Martin 457, 501; Tidman, Roger 467, 482; **NPL:** Packham, Chris 479; Varndell, Colin 478; **OSF:** 476, 477; Sanchez Alonson, Carlos 511; **PEP:** 465, 491; **Photos.com:** 498, 499; **Still Pictures:** Seitre, Roland 510.

All Artworks: Copyright Marshall Cavendish Corporation

Status

In the Key Facts on the wild species described in this publication, you will find details of appearance, name (both Latin and common name wherever possible), breeding, habits, and more. The status of an organism indicates how common it is. The status of each organism is based on the reference work *2001 IUCN Red List of Threatened Species*, published by the International Union for Conservation of Nature and Natural Resources (IUCN).

CATEGORIES

Extinct: When there is no reasonable doubt that the last individual of a species has died.

Extinct in the wild: When a group is known to survive only in cultivation, in captivity, or as a naturalized population.

Critically endangered: An extremely high risk of extinction in the wild.

Endangered: A very high risk of extinction in the wild.

Vulnerable: Facing a high risk of extinction in the wild.

Near threatened: Currently not threatened but likely to qualify for a threatened category in the near future.

Least concern: Includes widespread and abundant species.

Data deficient: When there is inadequate information to make an assessment of the risk of extinction.

Not evaluated: When a species has not yet been evaluated against the IUCN criteria.

Please note: The 1994 Red List categories included an additional category, lower risk/conservation dependent, which is still currently used for some species, but once they are all reassessed it will no longer be used:

Lower risk/conservation dependent: Species that are the focus of a continuing species-specific or habitat-specific conservation program targeted toward the species in question, the cessation of which would result in the species qualifying for one of the threatened categories within five years.

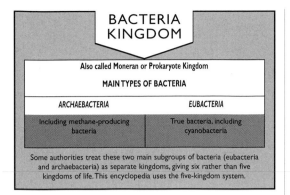

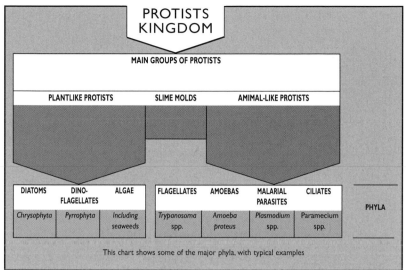

This chart shows some of the major phyla, with typical examples

KINGDOMS OF LIFE

In the eighteenth century, a botanist from Sweden named Carl von Linne (1707–1778; usually known by his Latin name, Carolus Linnaeus) outlined a system of classifying plants and animals. This became the basis for classification all over the world. Scientists use Latin names so that all plants, animals, and other living things can be identified accurately, even though they have different common names in different places. In this encyclopedia, Latin names are given for the key animal groups or species in an article. Linnaeus divided living organisms into just two kingdoms: plants and animals.

Scientists also classify living things into groups called kingdoms. The most familiar system of classification arranges organisms into five kingdoms of life: bacteria, protists, fungi, plants, and animals. Kingdoms are divided into decreasingly smaller groups called phyla or divisions, classes, orders, families, genera, and species. In the past, scientists placed organisms in a particular group largely based on what the life-form looked like, both externally and internally. Since the discovery of the role of genes (segments of DNA) and genetics, however, scientists have reconsidered many classifications. Some authorities think there should be at least thirty different kingdoms of life. Others think there should be six, with the bacteria divided into two kingdoms.

BACTERIA, PROTISTS, AND FUNGI

Bacteria are tiny, single-celled organisms called prokaryotes. Prokaryotes have no distinct nucleus. The nucleus is the DNA-containing control center of the cell. The life-forms in all other kingdoms are made up of eukaryotic cells, which do have a nucleus; only bacteria are prokaryotes. Bacteria are divided into two main groups: eubacteria ("true bacteria") and archaebacteria ("primitive bacteria"). Eubacteria, the largest group, includes the more familiar and common types of bacteria, such as cyanobacteria and *E. coli*.

Archaebacteria survive in extreme habitats, including very hot or saline ones. Some archaebacteria produce methane; others need sulfur to live. The latter are among the most thermophilic (heat loving) of the archaebacteria, surviving in temperatures higher than 122°F (50° C).

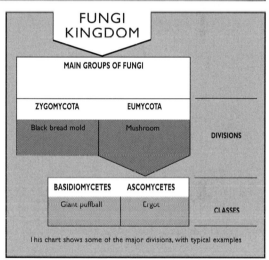

This chart shows some of the major divisions, with typical examples

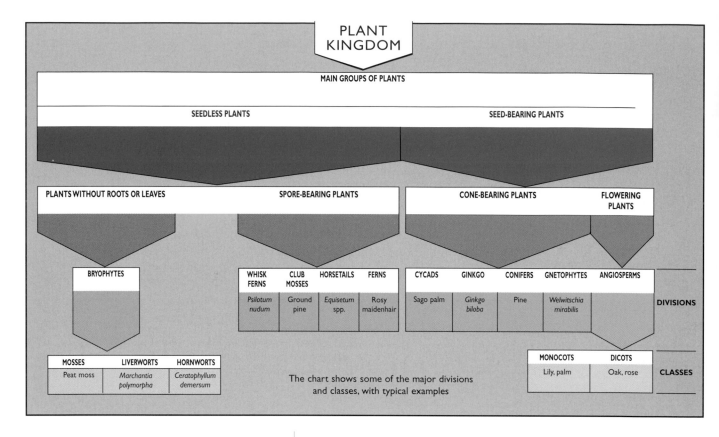

PLANT KINGDOM

MAIN GROUPS OF PLANTS

SEEDLESS PLANTS | **SEED-BEARING PLANTS**

PLANTS WITHOUT ROOTS OR LEAVES | **SPORE-BEARING PLANTS** | **CONE-BEARING PLANTS** | **FLOWERING PLANTS**

BRYOPHYTES	WHISK FERNS	CLUB MOSSES	HORSETAILS	FERNS	CYCADS	GINKGO	CONIFERS	GNETOPHYTES	ANGIOSPERMS	**DIVISIONS**
	Psilotum nudum	Ground pine	*Equisetum* spp.	Rosy maidenhair	Sago palm	*Ginkgo biloba*	Pine	*Welwitschia mirabilis*		

MOSSES	LIVERWORTS	HORNWORTS		MONOCOTS	DICOTS	**CLASSES**
Peat moss	*Marchantia polymorpha*	*Ceratophyllum demersum*	The chart shows some of the major divisions and classes, with typical examples	Lily, palm	Oak, rose	

Scientists have tended to classify organisms that are neither plant, animal, bacteria, nor fungi as protists. The protist (formerly protoctist) kingdom includes diverse and often loosely related species. Algae, such as diatoms and seaweeds, are plantlike protists. Amoebas are more animal-like protists.

Mushrooms, toadstools, and molds are all fungi. Once considered plants, fungi differ from plants in that they depend on other organisms for their food. Like plants, fungi have their own distinct kingdom.

THE PLANT KINGDOM

A plant is a living organism with rigid cell walls. Plants contain chorophyll, which is a green pigment that converts sunlight into energy by a process called photosynthesis. About 500,000 different species of plants have been identified. The plant kingdom (outlined above) consists of several divisions.

A plant division is similar to a phylum in animal classification. Each division represents a number of classes of plants that have certain physical features in common. As within other kingdoms, DNA analysis is providing botanists with information for revising traditional groupings, leaving plant classification uncertain.

Previously, the simplest plants were considered to be algae, a traditional grouping that includes both single-celled life-forms that live as part of the sea's minute floating community of plankton and multicellular seaweeds. Since they lack true plant parts, algae are now generally classed as protists.

Plants in one division, the bryophytes, lack roots, stems, and leaves that are found on plants in other divisions. Bryophytes include the mosses, liverworts, and hornworts.

The spore-bearing plants group comprises four divisions of the plant kingdom: whisk

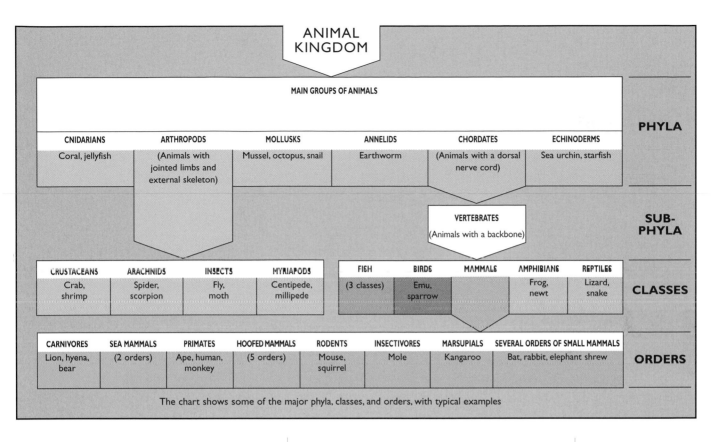

ANIMAL KINGDOM

MAIN GROUPS OF ANIMALS						**PHYLA**
CNIDARIANS	ARTHROPODS	MOLLUSKS	ANNELIDS	CHORDATES	ECHINODERMS	
Coral, jellyfish	(Animals with jointed limbs and external skeleton)	Mussel, octopus, snail	Earthworm	(Animals with a dorsal nerve cord)	Sea urchin, starfish	

VERTEBRATES
(Animals with a backbone) — **SUB-PHYLA**

CRUSTACEANS	ARACHNIDS	INSECTS	MYRIAPODS	FISH	BIRDS	MAMMALS	AMPHIBIANS	REPTILES	**CLASSES**
Crab, shrimp	Spider, scorpion	Fly, moth	Centipede, millipede	(3 classes)	Emu, sparrow		Frog, newt	Lizard, snake	

CARNIVORES	SEA MAMMALS	PRIMATES	HOOFED MAMMALS	RODENTS	INSECTIVORES	MARSUPIALS	SEVERAL ORDERS OF SMALL MAMMALS	**ORDERS**
Lion, hyena, bear	(2 orders)	Ape, human, monkey	(5 orders)	Mouse, squirrel	Mole	Kangaroo	Bat, rabbit, elephant shrew	

The chart shows some of the major phyla, classes, and orders, with typical examples

ferns, club mosses, horsetails, and ferns. All members of this group have two stages in their life cycle. At one stage, tiny reproductive structures, called spores, are released. These spores eventually grow into a new plant.

More complex plants reproduce with seeds. Four divisions reproduce with "naked" seeds in cones. Cycads, conifers, ginkgoes, and gnetophytes are all cone-bearing plants. Two classes, monocots and dicots, make up the largest division, the angiosperms, or flowering plants. Unlike cone-bearing plants, angiosperms reproduce with enclosed seeds in berries, nuts, or fruits.

THE ANIMAL KINGDOM

According to Linnaeus, animals were any life-forms that depended on other organisms for food and that could move around, generally using muscles. Within limits, this definition of an animal still works today. (All animals are multicellular, too; animal-like single cells are protists.) The animal kingdom is divided into many phyla. Most phyla contain life-forms loosely termed invertebrates—including microscopic organisms, sponges, corals, slugs, and insects. Invertebrates do not have the backbone and central nervous system that vertebrates have.

Each phylum or subphylum is divided into classes. For example, vertebrates are a subphylum that is divided into seven main classes: mammals, birds, reptiles, amphibians, and three classes of fish (bony fish, cartilaginous fish, and jawless fish).

Each class is further broken down into different orders. The mammal class includes the carnivores (meat eaters with cheek teeth), insectivores (insect eaters), primates (monkeys and apes), and marsupials (kangaroos, koalas, marsupial moles, numbats), among others.

COLOR GUIDE

AMPHIBIANS & REPTILES

BACTERIA, PROTISTS, & FUNGI

BIOMES, HABITATS & OVERVIEW ARTICLES

BIRDS

FISH

INVERTEBRATES

MAMMALS

PLANTS

Grasshopper

▲ **Grasshoppers are very good at dodging predators because they have the ability to leap huge distances relative to their body size. Their hinged legs give enormous thrust, and their claws help them grip when they land.**

Grasshoppers live in most parts of the world. They are usually well camouflaged, with coloring that blends into the background of grasses or other vegetation. Often, you can only tell that they are there because you can hear the "Screek, screek" of their legs rubbing against their wing cases when they are trying to attract a mate.

All insects go through a metamorphosis, completely changing their form as they develop from newly hatched larvae to adults. Many grasshoppers, however, go through a different kind of change in response to weather conditions. What seems like an ordinary grasshopper may turn into a locust.

You might think of grasshoppers as being green or straw colored, to blend in with leaves and grass stems. However, some look more like little flakes of rock, and there is one grasshopper, which lives in South America, that looks like a stick.

READY TO SPRING

When they are at rest, grasshoppers' legs are folded up at the back of their body, but they are ready to spring at any moment. Most species also have wings that help the grasshoppers increase the distance they can cover in a hurry. The wings are hidden away under hardened forewings, similar to the beetles' and earwigs' wings. Some species have brightly colored patches on their wings that are hidden away at rest. When the grasshoppers jump, the patches warn predators to stay away by flashing these patches or displaying spots that look like eyes.

Most grasshoppers live on grass and leaves, often in open habitats where there is plenty of plant material for them to chew on. Some species of grasshoppers have become infamous pests because of the way they suddenly increase their numbers and swarm over fields and cultivated land. These

KEY FACTS

Name

Grasshoppers and locusts belong to the Acrididac family; including the brown locust (*Locustana pardalina*) and desert locust (*Schistocerca gregaria*)

Range

Worldwide, but swarms are limited to subtropical, tropical, and warm temperate zones

Habitat

Grasslands and farmlands or areas of denser vegetation

Appearance

Up to 5 in. (12 cm) long, with short antennae (compared to crickets); coloring varies by species, according to surroundings; bolder coloring in swarming species

Food

Vegetation

Breeding

Male attracts female by rubbing his legs against his forewings; the female buries her eggs in the ground or decaying wood; the young larvae look like adults but cannot fly

Status

Not evaluated

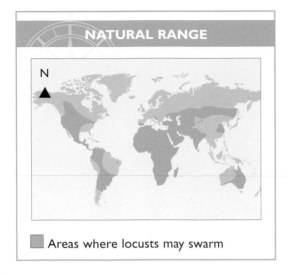

NATURAL RANGE

N

■ Areas where locusts may swarm

pests are found in semidesert areas, and their life cycle is quite different than that of grasshoppers in more temperate zones.

TURNING TO LOCUSTS

Grasshoppers that live in very dry areas are normally well disguised, eking out an existence on strawlike stems and stalks. However, even in these dry places, rains come from time to time (sometimes as rarely as once every five years). When the rains arrive, the grasshoppers suddenly become active. Young grasshoppers grow, changing form and developing much stronger coloring, often with brown, red, or cream patterning on their wing cases. The once harmless hoppers turn into locusts. They rise in a cloud and swarm, driven by the wind until they find fresh vegetation. Then they swoop and strip it bare. They continue to swarm, breeding as they go, for as long as they can find fresh shoots to devour. As the food supplies dwindle, the swarm dies out. Eventually the remaining grasshoppers

See also **Cicada, Cricket, Invertebrates**

may settle in an area where there is plenty of food. Or the swarm may be blown out to sea, where the locusts die.

BREEDING TIME

In those species that swarm, the breeding rate increases rapidly after the rains. Male grasshoppers attract their mates with their persistent call. After mating, the female lays her eggs (up to 200 at a time) in batches protected by a coat of foam. She has a short ovipositor (a stalk coming out of her abdomen) that she uses to lay the eggs well below the surface of the soil. Some species lay their eggs on plants, but not those that swarm.

Young grasshoppers look like and behave similarly to their parents, chewing on grass and leaping to safety, but they do not have wings. They molt three or four times before reaching adulthood.

▲ *Leaves, shoots, and other vegetation are completely smothered by a swarm of dark brown locusts (Locustana pardalina).*

Grebe

▲ *A grebe sits on its eggs, which have been laid in a floating nest. The male and female grebe build the nest from reeds and grass.*

KEY FACTS

Name

Red-necked grebe (*Podiceps grisegena*)

Range

Breeds on inland lakes, marshes, and ponds of Alaska, Canada, northern U.S., and Eurasia; winters along Pacific and Atlantic coasts

Habitat

Lakes, marshes, ponds, estuaries, and low coastlines

Appearance

17–22 in. (43–56 cm); the male has dark-gray-and-white breeding plumage, a black cap, white cheeks, and a dark red neck; the winter plumage is gray, with white on the head and throat; the bill is straight and black with a yellow tip

Food

Small fish, aquatic insects, crustaceans

Breeding

Solitary nesters; both parents incubate the 3–6 eggs for 22–23 days

Status

Least concern

The grebe is well adapted to its habitat. It dives and swims with ease, and with its thin neck and small head, it forms a spearlike shape when it plunges beneath the water. However, on land, it is very ungainly; its legs are so far back on its underside that it finds it difficult to stand upright, and it can hardly walk at all.

FEATHERED HUNTERS

There are 19 different species of grebes in the world, six of which are found in North America. Grebes live in both freshwater and saltwater environments. Many species of grebes migrate, breeding on inland freshwater lakes and marshes, and wintering on the coast or out at sea.

Grebes feed on small fish, shellfish, insects, tadpoles, and larvae. They dive deep and probe the bottom for their food, or they sit quietly, with their eyes on the water, ready to dart for fish as they swim past. Their strong, sharp bills are equally adept at catching small and larger prey. When they dive, they are able to see underwater. They have a third eyelid with a clear, thickened area in the center. This thick area is kept in front of the eye and acts as a correcting lens in the water. The third eyelid is called a nictitating membrane.

As grebes swim and dive underwater, they paddle with their lobed feet to propel themselves along. The feet have long toes that spread the grebes' weight when they walk over muddy surfaces. Because the ankles are very supple, grebes can twist their feet to steer themselves as they dive.

If they are threatened, grebes do have forms of defense. Crested grebes raise their crests to make them look larger and fiercer. The pied-billed grebe (*Podilymbus podiceps*) sinks slowly in the water by expelling air from its body and from under its feathers; it swims along with only its head above the water.

Grebes can also dive to escape a threat, and because they can dive so fast, they have been given the names "hell diver" and "water witch." Grebes rarely take to the air in self-defense. Becoming airborne is hard work; they have to pedal their feet across the surface of the water as they flap their wings for takeoff.

▼ *Soon after grebe chicks have hatched, they accompany their parents on foraging trips, piggyback style. The chicks are safer sitting on their parents' backs than they would be on their own in the nest; and they are safer clinging to their parents as they dive underwater than they would be swimming about on their own. This is a great crested grebe (Podiceps cristatus), which is found in many parts of the world—from Europe to Australia.*

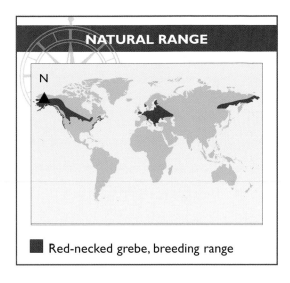

NATURAL RANGE

N

■ Red-necked grebe, breeding range

HUNTED FOR FEATHERS

One habit that is thought to be unique to grebes is that they eat their own feathers. It is not clear whether they do this in times of food shortage or if they do it routinely to recycle vital nutrients.

Their strong coloring and the fine quality of their feathers made grebes favorites with milliners, who used their feathers to decorate hats. This led to overhunting of grebes in the early twentieth century. They are now protected from hunting.

WATER BABIES

Grebes feed, sleep, and court on the water. During their courtship display, the male holds out his wings and puffs up his feathers. Pairs usually establish a small territory and nest on their own. They use grass and reeds to build a nest that floats on the water (or occasionally that nestles in the marshes). The parents share the task of sitting on the eggs. The striped, downy chicks feed on their parents' feathers, as well as on insect larvae and small fish.

See also **Birds, Duck, Goose, Waterbirds**

Groundhog

There is a special day in February called Groundhog Day. The story goes that on this day the groundhog comes out of its burrow after its winter hibernation. If it sees its shadow, it knows that spring has not yet arrived, and goes back to sleep for another six weeks. Therefore, if it's cloudy enough that a groundhog has no shadow on Groundhog Day, spring has truly arrived.

Groundhogs are large, stocky ground squirrels that are closely related to marmots. Also known as woodchucks, groundhogs are a familiar sight in woods and meadows throughout Alaska, Canada, and the eastern United States.

SOUNDING THE ALARM

Unlike most other marmots, groundhogs prefer to spend their time alone and do not live in large, sociable groups. They are diurnal (active during the day) and spend

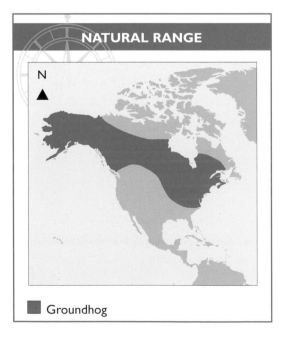

NATURAL RANGE

N ▲

■ Groundhog

much of their time resting and grooming in the sun or foraging for food, whistling loudly if they detect danger from predators. This alarm call, along with growling and chattering noises, may serve as a warning to intruders not to come any closer, or to other groundhogs that there is danger close by.

Groundhogs are mainly vegetarian. They feed on many kinds of grasses as well as berries, vegetables, and cereals. In particular, they seem to enjoy clover, alfalfa, peas, and beans. Indeed, they often cause much

▲ *While eating and foraging for food, groundhogs have to be constantly on the lookout against their enemies: coyotes and foxes. They often sit up on their hind legs to survey the land around. If they sense danger, they make a loud alarm call.*

KEY FACTS

Name

Groundhog or woodchuck (*Marmota monax*)

Range

Alaska, Canada, and the eastern U.S.

Habitat

Woodlands, meadows

Appearance

Large, robust body measuring 16–26 in. (40–66 cm), with a tail of 4–7 in. (10–17.5 cm); a thick, rough coat that is brownish gray with darker fur on limbs

Food

Vegetation including grasses and clover, fruit, cereal crops

Breeding

2–9 young born naked, blind, and helpless, about 1 month after mating; suckled for about 6 weeks; fully grown at 2 years

Status

Least concern

damage to farmland (and even gardens), and in some areas they are considered pests. As well as eating food growing on the ground, groundhogs have sharp claws that help them get a grip on the branches of trees and bushes, and they may sometimes climb to reach fruit before it has fallen to the ground.

The groundhog spends the night in its burrow. It digs this burrow itself, using its sturdy and powerful forelegs, which are equipped with strong digging claws. Outside the burrow there may be a pile of stones or soil, on which the groundhog stands to look out for enemies or as a place to bathe in warm sunshine on fine mornings or late afternoons.

WINTER HIBERNATION

Every year in October, the groundhog prepares to hibernate. Like many other squirrels, it collects food supplies that it hoards in its burrow in case it wakes up during the cold winter months. The groundhog sleeps for about five months, during which time its heartbeat drops from 80 beats per minute to four. It also breathes just once a minute rather than 28 times, and its body temperature drops as low as 40 to 45°F (4.5 to 7.5°C). In February or March (depending on how warm the weather is), the groundhog wakes from its hibernation.

YOUNG GROUNDHOGS

Within two months of awakening, it is the mating season. About a month after mating the female gives birth to a litter of two to nine young. The babies are completely dependent on their mother at first, for they are born naked, blind, and helpless. They have to suckle from their mother for about six weeks, by which time they have grown furry coats and are able to leave the burrow. Like other marmots, they are fully grown after two years.

See also **Mammals, Rodents, Squirrel**

▶ *A groundhog's burrow may have several entrances that are hidden from predators under a log or undergrowth.*

Grouper

Groupers are slow-moving fish that live on their own, usually close to the coast in tropical regions. They lurk in caves and around rocks, close to the bottom of shallow parts of the ocean. They are a big family of fish, and many grow to a large size: some are reputed to have grown to 1,000 pounds (450 kg), but there is no accurate record of such a weight.

GENTLE GIANTS

Some groupers, such as the giant grouper of western Australia, have a reputation for being quite vicious, and one species in Madagascar has a local name that means "man-eater." Groupers certainly have a huge appetite and have been known to stalk pearl and shell divers, like cats stalking mice. At other times, when divers come upon their hiding places, the groupers suddenly turn to face the divers in an effort to frighten them off. There is little evidence of any injuries caused by groupers, however, and divers who have worked for long periods under water in a limited area have reported that the groupers become quite friendly. Other divers have seen groupers being attacked by tiny fish known as threadfin butterfly fish. These fish move into an inviting hiding place, and when a grouper comes to claim the space, the butterfly fish turns its spiked back fin toward the grouper and swims backward. This behavior has driven huge groupers away.

KEY FACTS

Name

Giant grouper (*Epinephelus lanceolatus* and other species)

Range

Indian and west Pacific oceans

Habitat

Rocks with plenty of holes and caves

Appearance

Up to 12 ft. (3.7 m) long; mottled green and brown coloring; small scales; big jaws with long, strong, sharp teeth

Food

Carnivorous: crustaceans, mollusks, and some fish

Breeding

Spawns during the summer, possibly at full moon

Status

Vulnerable

◀ *This red grouper (Epinephelus morio), in the coral reefs of the Red Sea has stronger coloring than larger species such as the giant grouper.*

▲ The Malabar grouper (Epinephelus malabaricus) remains still while a cleaner wrasse goes to work. In general, groupers are not strong swimmers. They spend a lot of time just hovering outside their holes.

CLEANING STATIONS

Even more remarkable is the relationship between groupers and small fish called cleaner wrasse. These long, brightly colored blue-and-white-striped fish live in coral reefs alongside the groupers. Certain areas of the reef are recognized by the fish as cleaning stations. When a big grouper cruises in, a cleaner wrasse dances in front of it. The grouper hangs in the water, holding open its gill covers (through which it breathes) and its mouth. The little wrasse swims into the mouth, picking off pieces of dead skin, eating away at infections caused by fungi, and nibbling parasites. The wrasse even ventures farther into the huge jaws of the grouper and comes out through the gaping gill covers at the side of its head. Groupers appreciate the work of the wrasse and may come back to their cleaning stations twice a week.

WAITING FOR PREY

For a large part of its life, the well-camouflaged, dark-colored grouper just lurks around a hole, waiting for prey to drift past. Each grouper has quite a large territory and may have several holes or hiding places that it visits in rotation. It has a large mouth, and can extend its upper jaw to get a better grip on wriggling prey. It eats mainly shellfish and larvae, but larger groupers also attempt to catch other fish.

DOUBLE GENDER

The goliath grouper (*Epinephelus itajara*) of the Atlantic and Pacific coasts of the United States are huge, weighing up to 800 pounds (360 kg). They are particularly interesting because scientists believe that the young start off as males, able to fertilize females when they are a few years old, but later they change into fully functioning females and are fertilized by younger males. This creature is known as a sequential hermaphrodite. Scientists have proved that these fish can fertilize their own eggs, but the fish probably do this only as a last resort in the laboratory, and it is thought they do not do it regularly in the wild.

See also **Coral reefs, Fish, Invertebrates, Mollusks, Wrasse**

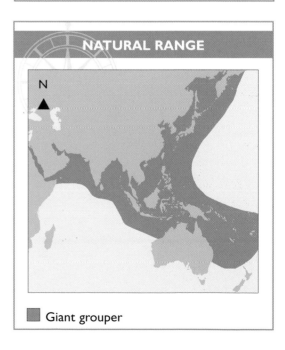

NATURAL RANGE

N

■ Giant grouper

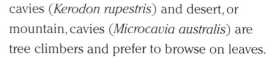

Guinea pig

Guinea pigs, or cavies, are the most common and widespread rodents in South America. They are small animals with large heads and short, robust bodies. There are 17 different species in the guinea pig family, which also includes agoutis, chinchillas, and capybaras. Cavylike rodents vary in size from rat-sized animals to as big as a large dog, and they live in a wide range of habitats.

ON THE GROUND AND IN THE TREES

Guinea pigs are herbivores (plant eaters), although different species have different feeding behaviors. The *Cavia* species are the guinea pigs most closely related to the domestic species. These ground dwellers spend their time feeding on grasses and herbs in moist grasslands. However, rock

▼ This mother and young are domestic guinea pigs (Cavia porcellus)—the best known species of all. These are no longer found in the wild but are popular pets around the world.

cavies (*Kerodon rupestris*) and desert, or mountain, cavies (*Microcavia australis*) are tree climbers and prefer to browse on leaves.

This kind of tree-climbing behavior may seem strange in such solid, sturdy animals; particularly in the case of rock cavies, as they do not have claws to help them grip branches or tails to keep their balance, but they do manage to climb to reach the leaves they prefer. They are also found on rocky outcrops and boulders, and there their large, padded feet prevent them from slipping on the smooth, rocky surface. Indeed, they are very nimble animals and can leap acrobatically between rocks.

LIVING ALONE

Not very much is known about the way guinea pigs organize their family life. However, they do seem territorial, and it is thought that male desert cavies defend ranges extending up to ¾ acre (0.3 hectares). Females stay within a smaller local area. Guinea pigs in the wild appear to prefer to live in groups of 10 individuals. Some, such as the *Cavia* species, are extremely aggressive toward each other even when there is no shortage of food in the area. Desert cavies live fairly peaceably with their neighbors in dry areas even where there is little food.

Despite their solitary existence in the wild, guinea pigs are quite noisy animals, communicating with a variety of sounds from squeaks through burbles, squeals, and chirps. Rock cavies may show that they are frightened or anxious by making a loud alarm whistle, and some species drum their hind feet on the ground.

Between one and three months old, guinea pigs are old enough to mate. After a relatively long pregnancy of two months, the female gives birth to a litter of two to four young. Although the father does not appear to help very much in raising the young, he may stay around the area to defend food supplies for the female and her babies.

Once the young become fully adult (at about three months old), they leave their mother. In some of the more aggressive species, they are actually chased away by their parents.

GUINEA PIG FARMING

Although the domestic guinea pig is no longer found in the wild, there are vast numbers of them in captivity throughout the world. They have been bred for their meat by native South Americans for at least 3,000 years, and they are still farmed for that purpose.

Guinea pigs are also bred for medical research in many scientific laboratories, and their cute looks and gentle nature

▲ *Male rock cavies have their own patch of rocks that make up their territory. They defend their colony, which may have up to 10 members.*

have made them popular household pets in many countries.

Most wild guinea pigs are common through South America. They are not badly affected by loss of habitat because they can adapt to new situations, and some may even live in areas alongside humans. However, rock cavies have been widely hunted for their meat and are found only in small pockets within their range.

THE BIGGEST GUINEA PIG

The Patagonian hare, or mara, is very closely related to guinea pigs. However, it is much larger than any of the other species of guinea pigs, measuring 27 to 29½ inches (69–75 cm) and weighing 20 to 35 pounds (9–16 kg). It is also shaped like a hare, with large ears that stand up straight and very long hind limbs that enable it to run at speeds of up to 18 mph (29 km/h).

NATIVE RANGE

N

■ Domestic guinea pig

See also **Capybara, Gerbil, Hamster, Rodents**

KEY FACTS

Name
Domestic guinea pig (*Cavia porcellus*)

Range
Originally Brazil and Paraguay in South America, before domestication

Habitat
Areas with thick vegetation

Appearance
A small, squat body measuring 8½–13½ in. (21.5–34 cm); color may vary from white through black, gray, or dappled white, orange, and black; a large head with rounded ears

Food
Plant matter

Breeding
A litter of 2–4 young are born just more than 2 months after mating; the young are fully adult at 2–2½ months old

Status
Least concern

465

Gull

The seashore would not be the same without the screech of gulls overhead. Gulls are familiar birds, with sleek feathers and a long, strong beak, often hooked at the end. There are some 45 species in the world. Most of them seem to have originated in the northern hemisphere, but many species have spread to all parts of the world except Antarctica.

FISHING BIRDS

All adult gulls have predominantly white undersides, so they are disguised against the sky when fish look up at them from below the surface of the water. Although most gulls are seabirds, many live on inland stretches of water, particularly during the breeding season. The most common, widespread, and typical seagull is the

▲ *The great black-backed gull (Larus marinus) has the smooth shape that is characteristic of the gull family. Scientists have discovered that the red spot on its beak is important in feeding the young: when the young peck the spot, the parent opens its mouth so that the young can feed on partially digested food.*

herring gull (*Larus argentatus*), which gets its name from its favorite food, the herring. Herring gulls are strong swimmers and superb fliers, making use of upward currents of air along the shoreline. They seem to hang almost motionless above cliff edges, riding the air pushed upward by onshore wind colliding with the cliff.

INLAND HABITATS

Flocks of herring gulls are now more and more common inland. They have learned many tricks to help them adapt to human environments. They scavenge for anything they can find on garbage dumps and take carrion or even sewage. The huge increase in numbers in the last few decades has made them commonplace in towns, where strenuous efforts have been made to stop them from nesting on and fouling buildings.

Herring gulls have learned some clever tricks to ensure that they get the freshest tidbits. They drop tight-lipped clams and tough sea urchins onto hard surfaces to crack them open, and in the winter they have been seen dropping mussels onto ice. They follow ships on the ocean for waste thrown overboard, and they follow plows, waiting for the worms and grubs that are exposed when the soil is turned over.

Even their digestion has adapted to their lifestyle. Any indigestible food that they swallow, such as fish bones and crab claws, they spit out in a pellet, rather than try to force it through the digestive tract. They are able to drink salty seawater as well as freshwater because they have glands above the eyes that excrete any excess salt.

NATURAL RANGE

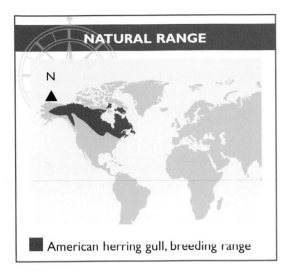

N

■ American herring gull, breeding range

Although they are useful scavengers in harbors and along beaches, where they clean up dead fish, crabs, and other sea animals cast up by tides, herring gulls also present some problems. Where they have become numerous they prey heavily on the eggs and

See also **Beaches and coasts, Seabirds**

young of terns, which has led to a decline in tern populations. They are also a problem near airports, where they have been known to collide with airplanes and cause accidents.

BREEDING SOCIETY

Herring gulls do not breed until they are several years old. They nest in colonies, building untidy nests on the ground or in trees. There are usually two to three eggs, which are incubated for around four weeks. Soon after hatching, the gull chicks peck instinctively at the red spot on their parents' bills, which induces the adult to regurgitate food to feed the young.

It is three years before the young get their adult plumage. They molt several times and grow new feathers, each set of which is more like that of the adult.

▼ *Herring gulls' mixed diet has enabled them to adapt well to human expansion. These gulls follow a boat, looking for tidbits in its wake.*

KEY FACTS

Name
American herring gull (*Larus argentatus*)

Range
Breeds across Alaska and northern Canada, south to the Great Lakes and along Atlantic coast toward North Carolina

Habitat
Islands, beaches, and mudflats; areas where there is human food

Appearance
23–26 in. (58–66 cm); medium to large gull, white head and underside, back light gray, and webbed feet; wing tips black with white spots; a heavy yellow bill with a red spot

Food
Omnivorous: marine life, plant and animal food, refuse, carrion

Breeding
Nests in colonies near water; the nest is a slight hollow in the ground, built up of weeds, grasses, and seaweed; usually 2–3 eggs laid May–August; they are incubated for 25–27 days; the young first fly 42–49 days after hatching

Status
Least concern

Halibut

The halibut is a flatfish. Its shape enables it to lie almost undetected on the ocean floor, ready to snap at other fish and sea creatures as they swim past. The development of flatfish is complicated and interesting to study.

EYED SIDE

The fish is flattened, like an angelfish, from side to side. The fins that lie along the edges of the body are the dorsal (back) and anal (belly) fins that in other fish are at the top and bottom of the body. However, if these bottom-living flatfish were simply regular fish lying on one side, they would have very restricted vision, with only one eye exposed most of the time. It might also be difficult for them to use their mouth if the mouth were half in the sand.

The halibut, like other flatfish, has a twisted skull, so both eyes are on the same side of the body and face upward. However, flatfish are not born with both eyes on the same side of the head. The larva emerges from a floating egg mass, which remains near the surface because the eggs contain oil. (Oil is lighter than water, so the eggs float.) The larva is like other fish larvae, barely more than a backbone, a head, and the remains of the yolk sac that was its food supply in the egg. It starts life swimming near the surface, feeding on plankton—tiny plants and creatures suspended in the water. As the halibut develops, it drifts inshore.

When the halibut is around two weeks old and measures around ½ inch (1.2 cm) long, things begin to change. It has already developed a flattened body, but now its head begins to change shape. The left eye (and it is always the left eye) moves up toward the angle of the halibut's head (where the bridge of the nose would be if it had a nose) and then gradually moves over to the other side

◄ **At two weeks, the tiny halibut lives near the surface. It still has one eye on each side of its head (left). Its left eye (shown as a dark shadow) begins to move up. ▲ In the adult fish, both eyes are on the right side or top of its body (above).**

KEY FACTS	
Name	Atlantic halibut (*Hippoglossus hippoglossus*)
Range	New Jersey north to Newfoundland, east to Iceland and Ireland
Habitat	Atlantic Ocean
Appearance	Grows to over 8 ft. (2.4 m); a laterally flattened body; jaws are well developed but crooked; left eye migrates to right side of body as it matures; the fins form a fringe around the body; green-gray coloring provides good camouflage; the sexes look similar
Food	Carnivorous, preys on other fish
Breeding	Over 2 million eggs are laid at a time and left to float near the surface; the larvae take a few days to hatch; the larvae change to resemble adult fish, and sink to the bottom
Status	Endangered

of its flat head. At the same time the mouth and nostrils twist so that they are on the top of the head—the side of the fish that is uppermost as it lies on the bottom.

READY TO ATTACK

As it develops, the halibut moves to deeper levels in the water until it comes to rest on the bottom. Because the fish has also drifted inshore, the sea is not very deep and the fish and shellfish there are the right size for its jaws. As it grows, it will gradually move farther out to sea in its hunt for bigger prey. Halibut, like other bottom-living fish, have no swim bladder (the organ that helps fish to move up and down through the water). Once they are on the bottom, they do not come up very far.

The color varies from green to gray or brown. In most species the underside is whitish, but the Greenland halibut (*Reinhardtius hippoglossoides*), which inhabits the colder North Atlantic, leaves the bottom for quite long periods to attack its prey. Its left (or under-) side has as much color as its right side. The Greenland halibut can also change the color of its upper skin as it moves from a pebbly to a sandy seabed. Its left eye is on the edge of its head, so it has some vision on its left side as it attacks.

HALIBUT AND HUMANS

Halibut are popular food for humans. They are related to other food flatfish such as flounder, plaice, sole, and turbot. Their size makes them popular: female Atlantic halibut (usually larger than males) can grow to 8 feet (2.4 m) in length and live for more than 30 years. Weights of as much as 700 pounds (about 320 kg) have been recorded.

See also **Fish, Oceans**

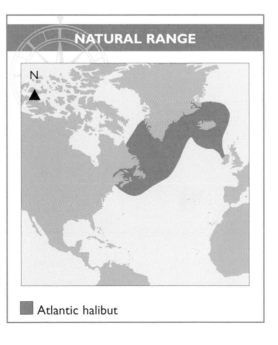

NATURAL RANGE

N

■ Atlantic halibut

▲ *The fringelike fins down each side of the halibut's body help it blend into its surroundings. If smaller fish, shellfish, or sand eels swim past, the halibut suddenly leaps to life to catch its prey. Although they spend most of their lives on the seafloor, halibut can swim by undulating their bodies up and down.*

Hamster

◄ *This tiny, fluffy Dzungarian, or dwarf hamster (Phodopus sungorus) is the smallest hamster, growing only to 2–4½ in. (5–11 cm) from head to tail, and weighing as little as 1¾ oz. (50 g). It is one of three species of hamsters found in Siberia, Mongolia, and northern China.*

The golden hamster (*Mesocricetus auratus*) is perhaps one of the most familiar pets kept in homes and schools throughout the Western world. However, this is just one of the 24 different species of hamsters that are found living wild in Europe, the Middle East, and parts of Asia.

Hamsters are small, furry rodents with large, bright eyes and long whiskers. They have an extremely good sense of smell, and can identify each other by scent. Hamsters also have excellent hearing, and they communicate by tiny squeaks as well as high-pitched sounds that humans cannot hear.

CARRYING AND STORING FOOD

Hamsters are generally herbivores (plant eaters). They eat all kinds of vegetation, including seeds, shoots, leaves, flowers, and many different root vegetables. However, the common hamster (*Cricetus cricetus*) may also occasionally hunt small creatures such as frogs, lizards, snakes, insects, mice, and young birds. If the area is quiet and there are no predators or competitors lurking nearby, the hamster may eat its food on the spot. Otherwise it carries it away to its burrow, either to eat it in peace or to store it for the winter. These stores will

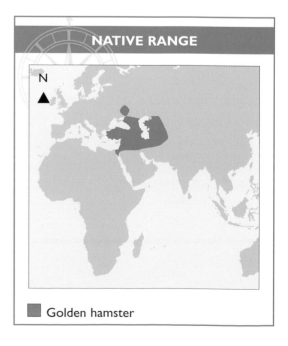

NATIVE RANGE

N
▲

■ Golden hamster

then be eaten during the cold months when it wakes up on warm winter days from its patchy hibernation.

Like other rodents, such as the chipmunk, the hamster has large cheek pouches. These are simply folds of skin stretching along the hamster's lower jaw from its cheeks down to its shoulders. They can expand to carry small items of food such as seeds. They are very useful for the hamster, which cannot always count on a regular food supply. When they are full, these pouches make the hamster's head seem twice its normal size. Hamsters may each collect as much as 30 pounds (14 kg) of food in their burrow to see them through the winter. The name *hamster* comes from the German word *hamstern*, which means "to store, stockpile, or hoard."

AGGRESSIVE BEHAVIOR

The time of day or night a hamster is active depends on the species. The golden hamster, for example, is usually nocturnal (active during the night), but the common hamster is mostly active during the mornings and the evenings when it is cool. Whenever hamsters are active, they are generally solitary and prefer to forage and rest alone rather than in large groups. Despite their reputation as good-tempered and gentle pets, in the wild they are often aggressive when faced with intruders. Some large species, such as the Korean hamster or ratlike hamster (*Cricetulus triton*), attack not only other members of the species, but also occasionally dogs and even people. One of the Korean hamster's defensive tricks is to frighten intruders away by standing up on its hind legs and shrieking loudly. This hamster grows to about 11 inches (28 cm) long.

NOT UNDER THREAT

The common hamster has long been hunted for fur, and larger species have been hunted for their meat in China. Some species are killed by trained dogs because of the damage they do to farm crops. However, a female hamster can produce up to 12 young in each litter. Perhaps because of this high breeding rate and their inaccessible habitats, most species are common and are not threatened.

See also **Chipmunk, Guinea Pig, Rodents**

▶ *Golden hamsters are favorite pets for children in North America and Europe. These hamsters are extremely successful at breeding. All the tame golden hamsters have descended from one female and her 12 young captured in northern Syria.*

KEY FACTS

Name

Golden hamster (*Mesocricetus auratus*)

Range

Originally Eastern Europe and Middle East down to northwest Iran before domestication

Habitat

Grassland and steppes

Appearance

Round furry body, measuring up to 7 in. (18 cm), with a small tail ½ in. (12 mm) long; thick fur that is colored deep gold or reddish brown on upperparts and paler below; large cheek pouches that extend from the cheeks down as far as the shoulders; large ears and dark eyes

Food

Nuts, seeds, shoots, leaves, flowers, root vegetables

Breeding

1 or 2 litters a year (in the wild), born 2 weeks after mating; the young are naked, blind, and helpless at birth, and are suckled for 3 weeks; they themselves are able to mate at just 6 weeks old

Status

Endangered

Hare

the arctic hare (*Lepus arcticus*), that can be found on the cold tundra of northernmost Canada, Europe, and Asia. It is so well disguised that it is difficult to see.

HIDING IN THE SNOW

During the winter months, when the landscape is covered in brilliant white snow, the arctic hare's fur is also white. This striking coat color gives it effective camouflage from its enemies, mostly arctic foxes and humans.

The winter may last for five to seven months of the year in the most northern parts of the hare's range. Then, in the spring, the snow begins to melt and the hare's winter coat stands out against the grass and rocks. Triggered by the change in temperature and amount of daylight, the hare molts. Soon it loses its winter white coat and is once again camouflaged, with a covering of grayish brown fur.

The arctic hare has adapted in many ways to life in a cold environment. Its feet are broad and covered in thick fur that insulates

Hares belong to a group of animals called lagomorphs, which means "hare shaped." Rabbits also belong to this family. Rabbits and hares look similar, with large dark eyes and long ears, but hares are generally bigger, with larger and more powerful hind legs. These legs enable hares to be very fast. When chased by predators, they can run at speeds of up to 50 mph (80 km/h).

Hares and rabbits are successful animals, and there are species found in every region of the world except hot, tropical rain forests and freezing polar ice caps. There is one hare,

▲ *Most arctic hares live in very open habitats, so they have to be constantly on the lookout for predators. They have long sensitive ears and large eyes set very high on their face so they can look sideways.*

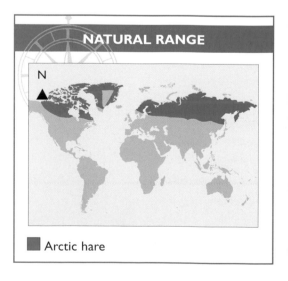

NATURAL RANGE

N

■ Arctic hare

them against the freezing temperatures and stops them from sinking in the snow as the animal runs. Its ears are also short compared to most hares. This may be because the arctic hare does not need to keep itself cool by losing heat from such a large surface area—as do species that live in hot, dry climates, such as the black-tailed jackrabbit (*Lepus californicus*).

NIBBLING AND GNAWING

Arctic hares are usually seen alone or in small groups. They mainly feed on small arctic plants and sweet-smelling herbs, although they will also eat dead animals (carrion) when they are available. Hares that live in coastal areas will eat seaweed. During the winter, they dig deep into the snow to find food, and they often nibble bark from young trees when other vegetation is scarce.

EATING TWICE

Hares have an inefficient digestive system to break down their food, so they have developed a special kind of feeding called refection. This means that they have to eat their food twice in order to get the most benefit from it. The first time they eat it, they digest half of it and produce small, soft black droppings.

They then eat these and absorb the rest of the valuable nutrients from it, eventually producing hard, dry feces.

HARES' HOMES

When they are not active, arctic hares rest in large hollows in the ground called forms. However, in parts of their range some actually use their strong claws to dig burrows in the snow. Arctic hares in Khatanga, Russia, dig complicated tunnels that measure up to 23 feet (7 m) long.

▲ *The arctic hare is the largest hare in North America. It is also called the mountain or blue hare. This picture shows an arctic hare in its brownish gray summer coat, which blends in with the sandy ground on Ellesmere Island, Canada.*

BOXING MATCHES

During the spring, mating season begins. At this time of year adult hares may often be seen "boxing." They stand upon their hind legs and hit out at each other with their forepaws. Contrary to the impression this gives of fighting for female attention, these are not rival males competing, but males attempting to court unwilling females.

LITTER OF LEVERETS

As well as fighting, the females constantly run away from their potential partners until they are ready to mate. About 7 weeks after mating, the female gives birth to a litter of 2 to 8 baby hares called leverets. When they are born, the young are extremely well developed. They are completely covered in fur, can see and hear immediately, and can move around very soon after birth. They become fully adult at about one year old.

See also **Mammals, Rabbit, Tundra**

KEY FACTS

Name

Arctic hare
(*Lepus arcticus*)

Range

Extreme northern parts of North America, Europe, and Asia

Habitat

Arctic tundra, above the timberline

Appearance

Large body of 2–2½ ft. (60–80 cm) with a small, round, furry tail of 1½–3¼ in. (4–8 cm); fairly short ears and large eyes; a thick, furry coat, white with black ear tips in winter; white below and grayish brown above in summer

Food

Arctic plants and herbs, young tree bark, carrion, seaweed

Breeding

1 litter of 2–8 leverets born about 7 weeks after mating; the young hares are very well developed at birth, with their eyes open and a good covering of fur; they are active almost immediately

Status

Least concern

Hawk

Hawks have very keen eyesight, muscular legs, and strong, usually rounded wings. The majority have hooked beaks and claws. Each of these characteristics is an adaptation for capturing and eating prey. Most hawks kill their prey with their claws and tear it apart with their beak.

DIVERSE LIFESTYLES

Hawks are relatively small birds of prey that, with eagles and vultures, belong to the family Accipitridae. They include true hawks, kites, and harriers. The true hawks are members of the *Accipiter* genus and include the sparrow hawks and goshawks. In North America the name *hawk* is also given to some members of the falcon family.

Hawks are a large group of birds that vary enormously in their hunting and feeding habits. Some hawks, such as the northern harrier, or marsh hawk (*Circus cyaneus*), hunt over open grasslands and marshes, searching for small mammals, reptiles, insects, and birds. These hawks have long, rounded wings and a long tail, which allow them to fly silently or hover for a short time over an area. Hawks also hunt by slowly flying low over the ground, although they can put on sudden bursts of speed. Their ears are especially adapted to listen for prey in tall, lush vegetation.

The harrier and crane hawk of Africa and South America live in woodland areas, where they hunt for small birds and other small creatures. These two hawks fly slowly, low over the ground, rather than hovering and diving. Unique among hawks, they have double-jointed legs that can bend both

KEY FACTS
Name
Red-shouldered hawk (*Buteo lineatus*)
Range
Eastern U.S. through southeast Canadian forest regions; also western California
Habitat
Woodlands
Appearance
Length 15½–24 in. (40–60 cm); rust color over neck, "shoulders" of wings, and throat; a long tail with gray and white bars; pale brown on the legs and flight feathers; males are smaller than females
Food
Small mammals, reptiles, insects
Breeding
Lays 2–5 eggs in nest of twigs and similar vegetation in trees.
Status
Least concern

◀ *Stalking through the lush vegetation, this red-shouldered hawk is hunting for prey such as lizards.*

backward and forward at the middle joint. This enables them to snatch small birds, mammals, and insects sheltering in cracks and crevices.

The flight of the goshawk (*Accipiter gentilis*) and the sharp-shinned hawk (*Accipiter striatus*), by contrast, is rapid. They usually take their prey on the wing, although they also seize animals from the ground or water. They are birds of woodlands and forests, with short, rounded wings and long tails. The goshawk catches all manner of small prey and will sometimes pursue it through trees and bushes by folding its wings to its sides and maneuvering with its long tail.

COURTSHIP AND BREEDING

Hawks make use of their excellent flying ability not only while hunting but also in courtship displays. The male and female northern harrier, for example, soar over their nesting site in the spring. Their wings may touch and they may rise to a great altitude. The male displays by climbing to heights of 200 feet (60 m) and then diving toward the ground with wings closed. Sometimes he spins around and then climbs again. He may loop-the-loop or fly upside down, repeating this whole performance over and over. Sometimes the female joins in.

When the eggs have been laid, the male brings food to the female. As he nears the nest, the female flies up to meet him. The male then drops the food held in his claws and it is caught by the female. This unusual behavior is known as the "food pass."

Male and female northern harriers' coloring are very different. The male is slate gray and

See also **Birds of prey, Eagle, Falcon, Kestrel, Osprey, Owl, Sparrow hawk**

white, with black at the tip of the wings. The female, on the other hand, is brown, with a checkered pattern of gray and black on the underwings and breast. Both have a white patch on the rump. Because of this difference, at one time the male and female were thought to belong to different species.

Like most small birds of prey, the marsh hawk lays several eggs. The nest of sticks, twigs, and moss is made in a hollow on the ground among tall grass, rushes, or other suitable ground cover. The four to six eggs are pale blue at first but fade to white. They hatch at intervals, and if conditions are poor and food is scarce, the younger chicks die. As the chicks grow, the male broods them while the female bird hunts. The female is larger than the male and can catch larger prey, providing more food for the nestlings.

▲ *This northern harrier has a wide wingspan, so its flight is strong and steady. Most of the feathers on the underside are pale, so the hawk does not stand out against the sky as it hovers for a short time looking for small mammals and other prey.*

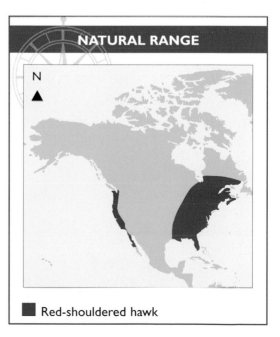

NATURAL RANGE

N ▲

■ Red-shouldered hawk

Hawthorn

FEATURES OF HAWTHORNS

Hawthorns belong to the rose family of flowering plants (Rosaceae). They are closely related to apples, which also belong in this family. Like wild roses, hawthorns have simple flowers with five separate petals. Hawthorn leaves are typically small, sometimes a simple oval shape but often with a jagged outline. Most species will grow to about 20–30 feet (6–9 m) high if not artificially trimmed.

As their name suggests, hawthorns grow sharp thorns on their stems. Longer and more needlelike than rose thorns, they can easily pierce human skin. The thorns of the cockspur hawthorn (*Crataegus crus-galli*) can grow more than 3 inches (7.5 cm) long.

MAY BLOOMS

Hawthorn flowers usually appear in May, and are sometimes called may blossoms. The white, pink, or red flowers grow in large clusters. Ornamental hawthorns often have deeper colors, and they have double sets of petals.

The flowers attract insects, which fertilize the plants by carrying pollen from one flower to another. After this the fleshy hawthorn fruits, called haws, start to develop. A haw is partly formed from the swollen top of the flower stalk, which grows around the developing seeds. The color of the ripe fruit varies between species, although it is most commonly red or orange. The group of species called Douglas hawthorns or black hawthorns (*Crataegus douglasii*), which are native to the northwest United States and Canada, have haws that are almost black.

Each haw contains one or more seeds, depending on the species. Hawthorn seeds

*▲ This Washington hawthorn (*Crataegus phaenopyrum*) is covered in red berries, called haws.*

Hawthorns are very common small trees and bushes that are widespread in the northern hemisphere outside the tropics. There are more than 1,000 species all together, and at least half of these are native to North America. Some kinds are commonly used as ornamental plants or hedges. Hawthorns are all classified in a single genus, *Crataegus*. Scientists find it difficult to decide exactly how many species there are in this genus, partly because different wild species sometimes interbreed to form natural intermediates (hybrids).

are stones—that is, each seed is protected by a hard woody outer coat. Ripe haws are often eaten by birds, and this hard coat helps the seeds pass unharmed through the birds' digestive system.

ECOLOGY AND USES

Hawthorns are tough plants that can survive harsh conditions. In nature, they can be found either beneath taller trees in forests, or sometimes growing on their own in dense thickets. They are very successful colonizers and can quickly take over abandoned fields, where their thorns help protect them against browsing animals. Hawthorns also have a wider importance in ecology. Their thorny branches provide year-round shelter and protection for many birds and small mammals.

Birds also build nests among the branches, as well as eating the hawthorn fruits in fall. Many insects feed on hawthorn leaves, whereas others collect nectar from the flowers.

HUMAN USES FOR HAWTHORNS

People have made use of hawthorns for centuries, and many folktales surround these

▼ *This close-up photograph of the scarlet hawthorn tree (Crateagus pedicellata) shows clusters of fruit.*

STATE FLOWER
MISSOURI

Name

Cockspur hawthorn (*Crataegus crus-galli*)

Range

From southern Quebec and Ontario to northern Louisiana, Alabama and northwestern Georgia, and west to Kansas

Habitat

Can grow in poor soils; prefers full sunlight

Reproduction

Reddish haws in fall, which remain on the tree throughout winter

Appearance

Small, widely spreading tree, growing to about 30 ft. (9 m), with very long thorns (except in some cultivated varieties)

Status

Not evaluated

plants. In England especially, hawthorn hedges were traditionally used to fence in livestock, and today these old hedges are a major habitat for English wildlife. Hawthorns are also grown in parks and gardens. Their fruits are sometimes used for food, as well as in herbal medicine. The wood is strong and hard, but hawthorn trees are not large enough for construction purposes.

See also **Flowering plants, Horse chestnut, Maple, Urban habitats**

HEATH

In late summer, heathland is a blaze of color, with purple heather and bright yellow gorse. The air buzzes with insects feeding on the flowers. From its perch on a gorse bush, a Dartford warbler (*Sylvia undata*) surveys the low shrubs then flits out to catch a spider. The bird's sudden movement startles a sand lizard, which scuttles away across a patch of bare soil.

▲ *A Dartford warbler sits on a gorse bush, waiting for invertebrate prey. The bird lives on dry heathland, with mature heather and dense bushes of gorse. The warbler nests in deep gorse or heather, and in snowy weather it will retreat to a patch of gorse.*

WHAT ARE HEATHS?

A heath, or a heathland, is made up of low shrubs, grasses, and herbs dominated by heathers (*Calluna vulgaris* and *Erica* species). Other tough shrubs like gorse (*Ulex europaeus*) and broom (*Cytisus*) form low bushes, and there may be a few birch trees (*Betula*) and pine trees (*Pinus*) dotted about. Heaths are usually on acidic, sandy soils that are poor in nutrients. They tend to form at low altitudes, often near the sea, where it is relatively warm and dry. Moors are similar to heaths, but they are usually in higher, cooler, wetter places.

Heaths are a habitat made by humans. Heaths began more than 5,000 years ago, when Stone Age people began to open forest clearings to attract wild animals. In areas where the soil was sandy and poor, heathland plants took over. Heathlands were useful to local people. They could graze animals there and cut heather for bedding and gorse for fuel. By grazing, cutting, and occasionally burning heathland, people kept heaths open and shrubby, and kept them from turning into woodlands.

CREATURES OF THE HEATHS

The low shrubby heath vegetation is home to a surprising number of insects and spiders. Bees and butterflies feed on nectar from heather flowers. Solitary sand wasps burrow into sandy soil. The sandy soil is also home to lots of ants. Many ant species live only in heaths.

Silver-studded blue butterflies (*Plebejus argus*) have a close relationship with ants. Ants collect a sugary liquid that is exuded by the butterfly's caterpillars. The ants then protect the caterpillar from parasitic wasps.

The dry heathland habitat suits lizards and snakes, which bask on bare soil. Mammals also use heaths. Deer graze on heaths, especially those close to woodland, and rabbits can easily dig tunnels in the sandy soil.

Heaths are important places for many birds. The low vegetation is good hunting ground for hobbies, kestrels, hobbies (*Falco subbuteo*) and other birds of prey. Nightjars make an eerie churring sound on summer evenings, while the wood lark sings its melodic song in spring.

WHERE DO HEATHS OCCUR?

Most true heaths are in northern and western Europe. Germany has one of the largest heaths, called Lüneberg Heath, and there are many smaller heaths in Britain.

There are similar dry, shrubby habitats in other parts of the world, but there the plants are not necessarily heathers. This shrubland or bush habitat occurs in different places, with different types of plants.

In the United States, coastal heathland on Nantucket and Cape Cod has grasses and shrubs, including lowbush

CONNECTIONS

Compare
Heath and SCRUBLANDS. Both have similar low-growing plants, but in true heathland, the plants are mostly heathers, gorse, and broom.

Find out more about species that live on heaths:

• ANT	• PINE
• BANKSIA	• PROTEA
• BIRCH	• RABBIT
• FALCON	• REPTILES
• GROUSE	• SAGEBRUSH
• HAWK	• VOLE
• HEATHER	• WARBLER

blueberry (*Vaccinium angustifolium*) and broom crowberry (*Corema conradii*). The endangered short-eared owl (*Asio flammeus*) and the northern harrier (or marsh hawk) hunt there for voles. Sagebrush scrub along the California coast has similar low heathlike plants.

Natural pasture (a result of summer fires) around the Mediterranean in France and Spain, has low plants with rosemary and other herbs. The Australian bush has acacias or wattles, banksias, and heatherlike plants (*Epacris* species)

Fynbos is a unique heathlike habitat that occurs only in South Africa. The word *fynbos* (FAEN-baws) means "fine bush." Many of the plants in fynbos have very fine, narrow leaves. Proteas (*Protea* species) are the exception. Their large leaves and bright chunky flower heads are a symbol of South Africa.

HEATHS ARE DISAPPEARING

People created heathlands for their own use. Now that agriculture is more intensive, and people do not need the products that heaths offer, heaths and their plants and animals are disappearing. Heaths that are not cut, grazed, or burned turn into woodland. Heathlands are also destroyed to make way for houses, factories, and roads.

◄ *A silver-studded blue butterfly feeds on nectar from a heather plant. Because it is a rich source of food, the heathland habitat is ideal for this butterfly.*

Heather

KEY FACTS

Name

Heather, Scotch heather, or ling (*Calluna vulgaris*)

Range

Asia, eastern North America, and northwestern Europe

Habitat

Heaths and moors

Appearance

Low-growing shrub, reaching from a few inches to more than 2 ft. (0.6 m) high; purple branched woody stem; small leaves that stay green all year long; pale pink, purple, or white flowers, ⅙ in. (4 mm) long, in upright spikes

Life cycle

Perennial

Uses

Brooms, baskets, and other utensils; ornamental; thatch

Status

Not evaluated

Heather is a low-growing flowering plant that is a familiar sight on heaths and moors in northern and western Europe and Asia. It is somewhat less common in eastern North America. On very dry, sloping ground, it forms a thin, spreading carpet just a few inches high. In sheltered places with more rainfall, it may grow into an upright, dome-shaped shrub up to 2 feet (0.6 m) high. The branching purple stems of heather gradually turn woody as the shrub gets older. Its small, tightly packed leaves remain on the plant all year round. Its tiny pink, purple, or white flowers form dense clusters on upright spikes.

CLOSE RELATIONSHIPS

Heather and its close relatives are the main plants that grow over the Scottish moors. Heather is an unusual plant in that it has no hairs covering its roots, so it cannot absorb water or nutrients from the soil. Special fungi take on the function of these root hairs. The fungi drink up the water and nutrients from the soil and inject them into the plant's roots with their long, threadlike hyphae (branching growths). The hyphae also help the plant absorb nitrogen—in an environment that is poor in nitrogen, this gives a big advantage to heather, which forms the main vegetation in the habitat.

In return, the fungus benefits by receiving carbon—the building block of life—from the heather. When a mature heather plant drops its seeds, the tiny seed capsules already carry hyphae with them. As a result, the new seedlings can absorb water and nutrients from the soil as soon as they germinate. This kind of relationship between a plant and a fungus is called a mycorrhizal association.

USES OF HEATHER

Heather is a perennial plant, which means that each individual lives for several growing seasons. If it is left undisturbed, the plant will continue to grow into a larger, spreading shrub, with more and more mature wood and fewer young shoots. However, the juicy young shoots are the main food of the red grouse (*Lagopus lagopus scoticus*), which lives on the moors of Scotland. Grouse shooting is a popular sport in Scotland, and landowners have to provide the grouse with plenty of young heather to lure them to their moors. The landowners periodically burn the older vegetation to allow new heather to grow.

As well as providing nesting material and food for birds, heather has also been used by humans for many years. For example, brooms and brushes can be made from the stems, baskets woven from the shoots, and huts and thatched roofs built from a mix of stems and mud. One of the biggest modern uses of heather, however, is as an ornamental garden shrub. Gardeners have to ensure that their soil is very acidic before they can grow heather successfully.

THE HEATH FAMILY

The term *heather* is often wrongly applied to some of the 3,400 different species of plants in the heath family (Ericaceae). However, *Calluna vulgaris*, which is also called Scotch heather or ling, is the only true heather. Heather has a different flower structure from heath. Heather's calyx—the fused sepals (cup-shaped, modified leaves) of a flower—and petals are of equal length and the same color. The flowers average ⅛ of an inch (4 mm) in length. Heaths have a very small calyx and a much larger, bell-shaped corolla (part of a flower that is made up of separate or fused petals) of different colors.

Heaths also have long, narrow leaves. The leaves of the heather curl back so much that they look triangular in cross section.

The heath family contains many other familiar plants that are found all over the world. Some, such as the azaleas and rhododendrons, are favorites in parks and gardens because of their glorious red, pink, purple, yellow, or white flowers. Other members of the family, such as the blueberries and cranberries (*Vaccinium* spp.), are popular because of their edible fruits. However, it is always important to be careful when eating wild berries. Many heath species are poisonous to both humans and domesticated animals.

See also **Grouse, Heath, Rhododendron**

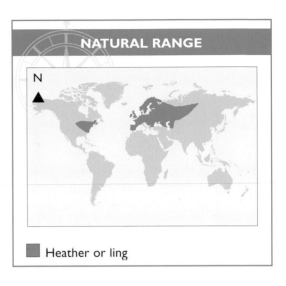

NATURAL RANGE

■ Heather or ling

▼ *Landowners frequently burn older, woody vegetation to make way for new heather to grow on the moors, where grouse hunting is a popular sport. Grouse feed on the shoots of young heather plants.*

Hedgehog

The western European, or common, hedgehog (*Erinaceus europaeus*) is one of the most recognizable animals in Europe. Its small, round body is covered with sharp spines similar to a porcupine, and it has an amazing ability to curl itself up into a ball when threatened to protect its face and soft underbelly. It has developed a close relationship with humans over the years, and it is often seen at dawn or dusk, foraging for food in suburban yards in western Europe.

A NIGHTLY WANDERER

The hedgehog is a nocturnal (active at night) animal and spends the day sleeping. Unlike its cousins the desert hedgehogs, the common hedgehog does not dig a burrow in the ground but makes a warm nest in the undergrowth, using grass and dead leaves. At night, the hedgehog spends its time traveling through its territory, which

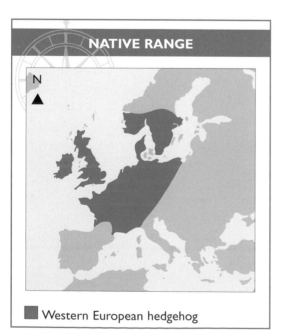

NATIVE RANGE

N

■ Western European hedgehog

▲ *Hedgehogs like to eat almost all kinds of invertebrates. This hedgehog is eating its favorite meal—an earthworm, which is one of the gardener's helpers. Despite this, the western European, or common, hedgehog has a good relationship with humans because it also feeds on many garden pests such as slugs, snails, and caterpillars that damage ornamental plants and vegetables.*

may be up to 85 acres (about 34 hectares). The hedgehog usually wanders quite slowly, although it is capable of running quickly when necessary—up to 4½ mph (7 km/h). With its long legs and sharp claws, it may climb small walls or fences from time to time. It is also a very good swimmer and does not hesitate before crossing a small stream or pond that happens to be in its path.

Hedgehogs prefer to forage for food alone. They do not gather in any kind of social or family groups. Although their eyesight is poor, they have a good sense of smell. They use this to best effect when foraging for food, snuffling along in the undergrowth with their long, flexible snout close to the ground. Their front legs are powerful and equipped with large, strong claws, enabling them to dig in the soil for their favorite items of prey.

Hedgehogs are insectivores (insect eaters), although they will eat all kinds of invertebrates (animals without backbones), including worms, slugs, and snails. They may also eat grass, leaves, seeds, fruit, birds' eggs, and nestlings.

Like many other small mammals, hedgehogs in cold areas may hibernate for about six months. They choose a spot in a tangle of undergrowth or brushwood and carefully construct a nest of leaves around themselves. Once asleep, the hedgehog's body functions slow way down to conserve energy. In warmer regions where the food remains plentiful, the hedgehogs do not hibernate. Desert hedgehogs that live in hot, dry countries spend the driest months in a state similar to hibernation. This state is called estivation.

BIRTH AND DEVELOPMENT

Once or twice a year, the female common hedgehog gives birth to her young about five to six weeks after mating. She rears them alone. Each litter comprises between 1 and 10 young, which measure about 2 to 4 inches (5 to 10 cm) and are naked, blind, and deaf when they are born. They already have about 150 tiny white spines, but these are covered by their skin so that they do not hurt the mother as she gives birth. Within a few hours, the spines pierce the skin and are soon supplemented by darker, more adult spines.

Once the babies are 14 days old, they can see and hear, their fur has started to grow, and they can almost roll into a ball. At 21 days, they are old enough to go on foraging trips with their mother. They are weaned at around six weeks old.

There are about 12 different species of hedgehogs found throughout Africa, Europe, and parts of Asia. Also in the same family are the moon rats and other gymnures. These are covered in fur and are sometimes called spineless hedgehogs.

Although many common hedgehogs are killed by motorists each year, their numbers have not been seriously affected, and they are not endangered. However, some moonrats are very rare and are threatened with extinction.

See also **Insectivores, Mammals, Porcupine**

▶ *The most recognizable feature of the hedgehog is its sharp spines, which are an extremely effective deterrent to predators. Whenever it is threatened, the hedgehog contracts its muscles so that its spines stick out. Then it curls up into a tight ball, protecting its underbelly from sharp teeth or claws.*

KEY FACTS

Name

Western European or common hedgehog (*Erinaceus europaeus*)

Range

Britain, western and central Europe, Mediterranean islands, introduced into New Zealand and United States

Habitat

Deciduous forests, open woodlands, grassy heaths, scrub

Appearance

A small, rounded brown body measuring 8–11½ in. (20–29 cm) and covered in dense, sharp spines; dark eyes; small ears; a long, flexible snout

Food

Worms, slugs, snails, caterpillars, insects; occasionally carrion and birds' eggs or nestlings

Breeding

1 or 2 litters per year; containing 1–10 (usually 4–7) young; the babies are naked, blind, and deaf at birth, with spines under the skin; they are suckled by their mother until they are around 6 weeks old

Status

Least concern

Hemlock

Hemlock (*Conium maculatum*) is one of the most poisonous plants in North America. From its outward appearance it might not be regarded as poisonous, because it looks very similar to wild carrot and parsnip plants. Hemlock belongs to the parsley family (Apiaceae, or Umbelliferae).

A POISONOUS PLANT

The toxic substance within the plant's tissues is a chemical called coniine, which causes breathing difficulties. All parts of the plant are poisonous, but the seeds contain particularly high concentrations of coniine. Hemlock is so poisonous that it was once used as a method of execution. For historical reasons, it is commonly called poison hemlock. The ancient Greek philosopher Socrates (c.470–399 B.C.E.) was sentenced to death by drinking hemlock.

LIFE CYCLE

Poison hemlock is an example of a biennial herb. (The term *biennial* refers to any plant that completes its life cycle over two years.) During the first year of its life cycle, poison hemlock germinates from seed and grows steadily. In the second year, flowers, fruits, and seeds are formed during the reproductive stage of the plant.

Poison hemlock is native to Europe, temperate areas of western Asia, and coastal regions of northern Africa. However, it has been introduced to the eastern United States, southern Canada, and many other countries. Hemlock grows along roadsides, at the edges of streams, and on waste ground. It is a fairly tall plant, reaching up to 8 feet (2.5 m) tall when it is fully grown, with a characteristic, fetid smell. Herbs are plants such as poison hemlock whose stems do not become woody as the plant grows. The stems remain green and soft and die back completely at the end of the life cycle.

The hollow, grooved stem and branches of poison hemlock are usually covered with purple spots, so the plant is sometimes called spotted parsley. The green fernlike leaves are divided into several narrow, saw-toothed segments. When the plant flowers, it almost looks as if it is carrying tiny parasols. Small

◄ *The characteristic parasol-like flowers of the deadly poison hemlock are a common sight in many parts of the world.*

KEY FACTS
Name
Poison hemlock (*Conium maculatum*)
Range
Europe, western Asia, and northern Africa
Habitat
Fields, riverbanks, roadsides, woods, and on waste ground
Appearance
Large herb, up to 8 ft. (2.5 m) high; ridged, hollow stems, with purple spots; green, segmented leaves; clusters of white flowers ½ in. (2 mm) across, arranged like parasols at the top of the stems, with 10–20 spokes; small ridged fruits
Life cycle
Biennial
Uses
Source of coniine
Status
Not evaluated

white flowers are clustered together to form umbrella-shaped heads that are up to 2 inches (5 cm) across.

EDIBLE RELATIVES

Poison hemlock looks very much like its harmless relative, cow parsley (*Anthriscus sylvestris*). However, on close examination the two plants look different. The stems of cow parsley have a covering of fine hairs, while those of poison hemlock are smooth. The parsley family also contains many edible plants, especially root vegetables such as

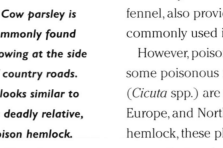

▼ *Cow parsley is commonly found growing at the side of country roads. It looks similar to its deadly relative, poison hemlock. Unlike poison hemlock, however, fine hairs cover the stem of cow parsley.*

carrots, celery, and parsnips. Many plants in this family, including anise, coriander, dill, and fennel, also provide flavorful spices that are commonly used in cooking.

However, poison hemlock also has some poisonous relatives. Water hemlocks (*Cicuta* spp.) are poisonous weeds of Asia, Europe, and North America. Unlike poison hemlock, these plants are perennials, which means that each individual lives for several growing seasons.

A COMMON NAME

Poison hemlock is not to be confused with pine trees from the group (genus) *Tsuga*, which are also known as hemlocks. These large coniferous (evergreen) trees, which are native to North America and central and eastern Asia, are not poisonous at all. Humans make use of these trees in many ways: a substance called tannin, found in the bark of the trees, is used to tan leather; the wood is often used as timber; and some species are popular as ornamental plants.

See also **Buttercup, Dandelion, Deadly nightshade, Flowering plants, Foxglove**

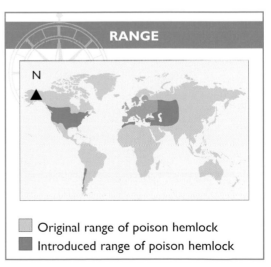

RANGE

N

☐ Original range of poison hemlock
■ Introduced range of poison hemlock

Hermit crab

◀ *This hermit crab is searching for a new home that will protect its soft body.*

Hermit crabs are found throughout the world in shallow coastal waters. Their legs and claws look like those of other small crabs, but they are unusual in that they do not have their own shell. Out of their shells, hermit crabs look more like lobsters than crabs, but they do not have the lobster's armor to protect their soft abdomen (rear body).

FINDING A HOME

To compensate for their lack of armor, hermit crabs live inside discarded shells of sea snails. They corkscrew their tails around the spiral of the shell, which they grip with their back legs. Once they reach adulthood, hermit crabs start their search for the right-sized home. In most parts of the world, they choose whelk shells because their tapering shape seems to suit the shape of the hermit crab. However, in parts of the Indian and Pacific Oceans, there are no whelks, and the hermit crab goes for cone shells instead. The young adults can be seen inspecting different shells. They seem to be able to recognize shells that they have checked out already and will come back to them several times. However, when they find a shell that they have not inspected before, they are clearly much more excited and explore it carefully. Hermit crabs have been found living in coconut shells, bamboo stems, and even glass jars.

When they find a shell of a suitable size, they back into it. For complete protection, they can hold their right front limb (larger than the other limbs) over the mouth of the shell. When the crab needs to move to hunt for food, it simply drags the shell along with it, clawing its way forward with its front limbs. From time to time, the hermit crab has to move to a newer, larger shell, since it continues to grow for many years. Like other crabs, they also undergo molting at regular intervals, which may or may not coincide with a change of shell.

LIVING TOGETHER

Even more remarkable, perhaps, is the way in which hermit crabs develop working relationships with other creatures. The most spectacular and successful relationship of the hermit crab with another animal is with sea anemones. The hermit crabs benefit in several ways and actually go out to collect the anemones. They use their claws to pick them from rocks or other shells and "plant" them on the outside of their own shell. The waving tentacles camouflage the hermit crab and, because they are poisonous, provide protection from predators such as fish and larger crustaceans.

At the same time, the anemones benefit because the crab constantly stirs up the ocean floor, and the tentacles of the sea anemones can pick up food scraps and plants that are too small for the crab to eat. The partnership of a hermit crab and its sea anemones is long term. When the crab is ready to move to a larger shell, it picks all the anemones off the old one and brings them to the new one. Hermit crabs have been seen moving close to other hermit crabs to poach their sea anemones.

Some other types of hermit crabs live inside sponges. This may have happened because the sponge had taken over and engulfed the crab's shell, but many sponge hermit crabs do not bother with a shell at all.

See also **Arthropods, Crab, Sea anemone**

◄ *This hermit crab, with its pink legs and head showing at the opening of the green shell that it has moved into, has disguised itself with three colorful sea anemones.*

Heron

Herons are slim wading birds with long thin legs, and subtly colored plumage. They are skilled hunters, and can be seen poised at the water's edge, ready to catch any passing fish with their daggerlike beak. There is a large range of color and size across the 60 or so species. The smallest, the little zigzag heron (*Zebrilus undulatus*), is 1 foot (30 cm) long; the largest is the goliath heron (*Ardea goliath*) of Africa and Asia, which may be as long as 55 inches (140 cm).

These lean, long-legged birds are often mistakenly called cranes, but cranes and herons are not closely related. The great blue heron (*Ardea herodias*) is the largest of the North American herons. It is majestic in flight, with its neck folded and long legs trailing behind.

▼ *This great blue heron has caught a sizable meal—a catfish. After catching it by clamping it firmly in its beak, the heron struggles with it and swallows it whole.*

KEEN HUNTER

The great blue heron is a solitary feeder, each bird maintaining a territory in which its prey is not disturbed by other herons. Although it belongs to a family known as day herons, the great blue fishes by day and by night, being most active just before dawn and at dusk. The great blue heron stands motionless in shallow water waiting for prey to come within striking distance. It usually catches smaller fish crosswise in its bill and swallows them whole; but it spears large fish.

Herons have been known to underestimate the size of their prey. Some have been seen choking to death while trying to swallow fish that are too large. They have no means of chewing up their food before they swallow it. Along with fish, herons will eat small mammals such as rats, mice, shrews, ground squirrels, and pocket gophers. Sometimes they catch lizards, frogs, and aquatic insects.

DISPLAY TIME

Breeding adult herons have ornate plumes on their head, neck, and back. In elaborate courtship displays, they fluff up their feathers, shake twigs, and pose in front of each other, sometimes making little flights to draw attention to themselves.

In great blue herons, there is no single pattern for nest building. Some pairs remain solitary, others group together to form

▲ *This great blue heron stands by a low dam, scanning the water for fish. Here, the water is stirred up and full of oxygen, which attracts fish.*

colonies of anything from a handful of pairs to hundreds of birds. The nest may be on the ground, on rock ledges, on sea cliffs, or in treetops. The pairs build flat, flimsy platforms of sticks about 18 inches (45 cm) across, and many come back to the same nest year after year. In subsequent years, they add to and strengthen these nests until older nests reach 3 to 4 feet (more than 1 m) across.

The female great blue usually lays four eggs, although there may be as many as seven. The eggs are turned regularly by the parent at the nest. After hatching, both parents feed nestlings on insects and fish they have caught, which they bring back up to their mouths partially digested.

RELATED SPECIES

Herons are found in many parts of the world and are related to egrets and bitterns. All have the same long beak, and usually a long neck and legs and high shoulders. The cattle egret (*Bubulcus ibis*), unlike most herons, feeds in fields and grasslands (particularly among cattle) rather than in rivers, lakes, or marshes.

NATURAL RANGE

N ▲

■ Great blue heron

See also **Birds, Crane, Limpkin, Waterbirds**

KEY FACTS

Name

Great blue heron (*Ardea herodias*)

Range

Lives year-round across United States and south to Central America

Habitat

Marshes, swamps, shores, tidelands

Appearance

42–52 in. (105–130 cm), with a 7-ft. (2-m) wingspan; a lean, blue-gray wading bird; a white head with a trailing crest; an all-white form lives in southern Florida; long legs and neck and a daggerlike bill; both sexes look similar

Food

Mainly fish; also small mammals, reptiles, amphibians, and insect larvae

Breeding

Builds untidy nest; 3–7 (usually 4) eggs are laid March–May; the male and female incubate the eggs for 25–29 days, rolling them over every 2 hours; the young start to fly 2 months after hatching and leave the nest after 3 months

Status

Least concern

Herring

Herring are a well-known species of fish because they are an important food source for humans. The common herring (*Clupea harengus*) is found in the northeastern part of the North Atlantic Ocean, where it has been fished for centuries. Similar species are found in the Pacific Ocean, from Alaska to San Diego and across to Japan and Korea. Herring are an excellent example of a food-chain link. They feed on plankton, the tiny animals and plantlike single-celled algae that float in the seawater. The herring, in turn, are eaten by larger fish and mammals, so the nutrients from the plankton are passed to larger species in the chain.

SCHOOLS ON THE SHELF

Herring live in deep water, but they do not swim through the great ocean troughs. They live on the continental shelf, which is a continuation of the land beneath the sea that often links coastal islands to the mainland. There is a continental shelf that extends across the North Atlantic, linking

▲ *The herring is a streamlined, muscular fish with a single dorsal fin. Its lower jaw is longer than its upper jaw, so it can scoop up plankton.*

North America to Greenland, Iceland, and the British Isles. To the east of the British Isles, the North Sea lies on another continental shelf. This is a rich fishing ground, although restrictions have been imposed to protect the fish supply. Similarly, Alaska and the Aleutian Islands are linked under the Bering Sea to China, and Japan by a continental shelf. This is the area where the Pacific herring (*Clupea pallasii*) is found. It too has been heavily fished by the Japanese and Russian fishing industries.

The waters of the continental shelf are rich in the herring's food, which is plankton—plantlike cells and animals that are so small they can be seen only with a microscope. Herring feed by taking plankton-rich water into their mouths and filtering out what they need. Their mouths, which are small and weak, have a series of long bristles around the front called gill rakers. As the water is forced out of the mouth, the gill rakers catch the plankton.

One of the reasons herring are so easily caught by modern fishing boats is that they swim in vast schools. Although the fish reach speeds of up to 3½ mph (5.5 km/h), trawlers are able to scoop thousands of them up in their long, sacklike nets.

SAFETY IN NUMBERS

The herring faces many enemies besides people. On the continental shelf there are many large fish and sea mammals, as well as birds, waiting to snap up a nutritious meal. The herring's predators include dogfish, salmon, whales, seals, and seabirds. Sharks have been known to attack herring that have already been caught in trawl nets.

In an attempt to avoid predators, herring swim in schools more than half a mile (1 km) across, which may contain many millions of individuals. If a big predator approaches, those on the outer edges of the school dart inward, taking refuge in the center of the school. If the predator charges, the herring

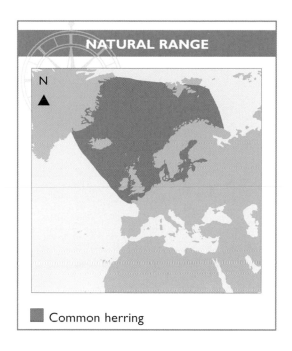

NATURAL RANGE

N ▲

■ Common herring

◀ *These tiny dwarf round herring (Jenkinsia lamprotaenia), in the warm waters of the Caribbean Sea, move through the encrusted rocks. Many small members of the herring family, such as sprats and sardines, are caught for food. However, these fish, at 2½ in. (6.5 cm), are too small for human consumption. They are chased and eaten by larger fish.*

flee from it, creating a clear tunnel through the school. As the predator attacks, the herring dart in all directions, confusing it. The predator is even more confused by the fact that all the herring in the school look almost identical, so it cannot focus on a particular member of the school or concentrate energy on catching weak or small fish.

SPAWNING SEASON

During the winter months, herring live in the southern part of their range. When the weather warms up, spring comes to the underwater world of plankton. As plankton become active farther and farther north, the herring follow them. They may travel hundreds of miles each year between their winter feeding grounds and their spawning grounds. The females leave a sticky mass of eggs on the seabed, where they are fertilized by the males. The eggs hatch into new schools of herring.

See also **Cod, Fish, Oceans**

Hippopotamus

The hippopotamus (hippo) looks like a large, round hog with a bulky body and short, stubby legs. The name *hippopotamus* means "river horse" in Greek—perhaps a rather odd name for such a bulky creature. However, when a hippopotamus is in the water, it is remarkably graceful, just like a horse is on land. The common hippopotamus (*Hippopotamus amphibius*) spends much of its day in water.

FAST AND DANGEROUS

Even on land, hippos are surprisingly nimble. They can climb up steep, slippery banks, then take off and charge at speeds of up to 20 mph (32 km/h). Their speed and their extraordinarily strong jaws and teeth make hippos extremely dangerous. In many countries, they are second only to crocodiles in the number of people they kill.

Hippos must stay in the water during the day, mainly to keep cool (they have no sweat glands), but also because their skin is so sensitive that it would get burned if exposed to the hot tropical sun. Yet, like many other African animals, hippos eat grass. Each night they climb out of the water and march up the banks and out onto the plains. There they spend five or six hours grazing, using their hardened lips rather than their teeth to pluck and rip the grass. The hippo has a particularly efficient digestive system and eats relatively little. It consumes 1 to 1.5 percent of its body weight daily. By comparison, a domestic cow eats about 2 percent of its weight each day.

During the day the hippo rests while submerged in the water. The ability to stay underwater is related to a hippo's size. Young animals can stay submerged for only 30 seconds, but by the time they are adults they can stay under for up to five minutes. It is essential that adults are able to stay underwater for such a long time because

▼ *These male hippos are defending their river territories. Such fights are often very vicious, and many competitors sustain serious injuries.*

KEY FACTS
Name
Common hippopotamus (*Hippopotamus amphibius*)
Range
Most of west, central, and southern sub-Saharan Africa
Habitat
Rivers and lakes in grasslands
Appearance
Large, barrel-shaped body, measuring up to 16 ft. (5 m) long and weighing 7,000 lb. (3,200 kg); dark brownish gray upperparts with lighter underparts; large, flattened jaws; eyes, nostrils, and ears on top of a large, rounded head
Food
Grass
Breeding
Single calf (rarely two) born on land or in shallow water; the calf weighs under 100 lb. (45 kg) at birth and is suckled for 6–12 months
Status
Least concern

mating takes place in the water, and often the female is completely submerged during courtship.

GUARDING THE BANKS

Hippos generally live in very loose groups. The only social bond that is consistent is the one between a mother and her calf. While males defend their territories, both in the water and in the grazing areas along the riverbanks, females move up and down the river, frequently changing groups.

The male defines his territory by marking it with his feces. When in the water, he sprays it by whipping his tail back and forth; while on land he leaves little piles called middens. These not only mark his territory, but also alert other males to his presence.

Male hippos are fairly aggressive, and fights often break out between individuals. These fights, usually evenly matched tests of strength between younger males, begin with the competitors opening their jaws wide to form an angle of 150 degrees. They then clash their lower jaws together, which can break their teeth. Much biting is also involved, and all hippos have very thick skin on their hindquarters that shields them against bites from their competitors. Even so, scars are a common sight on male hippos.

CONSERVATION

Hippos were once found from the Nile River all the way south to the Cape of Good Hope. They are still common throughout much of sub-Saharan Africa but face a continual threat to their numbers from hunting. Their teeth are a fine substitute for ivory, their meat

See also **Hoofed mammals, Mammals**

is good to eat, and their hides are tough and durable. Although the common hippo is not currently threatened, its numbers are declining.

PYGMY HIPPOPOTAMUS

The pygmy hippo (*Hexaprotodon liberiensis*), of western Africa, is a smaller version of the more common hippopotamus. It weighs only 600 pounds (272 kg). This species is vulnerable. Over much of its range, people have ripped up the forests, plowed grasslands, polluted the rivers, and removed the grassy vegetation the hippo needs to survive. Industrialization and the resulting pollution give pygmy hippos (and in many areas, common hippos) little chance to recover their lost habitat.

▲ *Although hippos are well adapted to life in the water, they spend much time on dry land. However, they only venture out of the river to feed once the sun has set.*

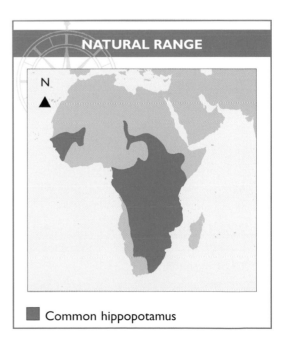

NATURAL RANGE

N
▲

■ Common hippopotamus

Holly

in both temperate and tropical climates around the world, belongs to a family called the Aquifoliaceae. One South American species, the yerba maté (*Ilex paraguariensis*), is a shrub that grows to around 20 feet (6 m) tall. It is famous for its evergreen leaves and can be made into a tea. Many other hollies shed their leaves in the fall.

There are two main species of hollies commonly found in North America. A native species, known as the American holly (*Ilex opaca*), grows along the eastern and southeastern coast, from Texas and Florida up to Massachusetts. English holly (*Ilex aquifolium*) was introduced from Europe and Asia, and it grows down the western coast, from British Columbia in Canada to California. Both of these species look very similar, but the leaves of the English holly are darker and glossier than those of the American holly.

With its sharp, prickly, dark green leaves and brilliant red berries, holly is second only to the Christmas tree in its popularity as a seasonal decoration in Western countries. Holly is often seen growing as an ornamental hedge, shrub, or tree in gardens and parks.

There are around 400 species of hollies, 13 of which are native to the United States. This group of trees and shrubs, which grows

▲ *Only female holly trees develop the brilliant red juicy berries; male trees do not bear any fruits at all. Although the fruits are eaten by birds such as thrushes, they are extremely poisonous to humans.*

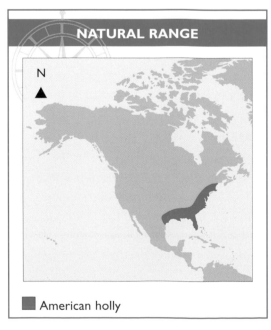

NATURAL RANGE

N

▲

■ American holly

LUCKY TREES

Many centuries ago, people thought it unlucky to cut down a holly tree or shrub, which was said to prevent death and keep away evil spirits. As a result of this taboo, while all the other hedge plants might get trimmed down, the fortunate holly was left to grow into a full-sized tree.

If they are not clipped and shaped to form part of a garden hedge, hollies will grow into tall, cone-shaped trees. The American holly commonly reaches between 10 and 40 feet (3 and 12 m) in height, but the tallest holly is *Ilex guianensis,* or the maconcona, of Central America and northern South America, which may grow to 130 feet (40 m) high.

FENDING OFF PREDATORS

There are many varieties of holly, with leaves in a range of colors, shapes, and sizes. For example, a variety of English holly called Lawsonia has oval-shaped, almost smooth-edged leaves, colored green in the center and yellow around the edge. Leaves with this kind of two-tone coloring are called variegated. Most hollies have deep green leaves, with sharp spines around their edges. These prickles protect the plant from large, browsing plant eaters (herbivores). The mat, dark green leaves of the American holly are between 2 and 4 inches (5 and 10 cm) long. Their edges are less spiny than those of English holly leaves, which can be 1 to 4 inches (2.5 to 10 cm) long.

The bark of the holly tree is green, but it soon becomes smooth and gray with age. The hard, heavy, white or greenish white wood beneath is sometimes used for wood engravings as well as for making furniture and musical instruments.

In spring, white four-petaled flowers appear on the holly plants, with male and female flowers growing on separate trees. Plants that have male and female flowers on separate plants are called dioecious plants. Holly flowers have a delicate perfume to attract insects. As the insects fly from tree to tree, they unknowingly transfer pollen from the male holly flowers to the female ones.

Once the flowers have been pollinated and fertilized, the female holly trees develop juicy fruits containing several seeds. (Male holly trees do not bear any fruits at all.) These are usually in the form of red berries, although in some varieties they may be black, golden yellow, or orange. The fruits are particularly attractive to perching birds such as thrushes, which feed on them during the winter months when other food is scarce. However, if eaten by humans, holly berries can cause violent nausea.

See also **Flowering plants, Temperate forests**

◀ *The holly blue butterfly (**Celastrina argiolus**) lays its eggs on holly leaves. The eggs hatch into caterpillars, which then eat the leaves.*

KEY FACTS

Name
American holly
(*Ilex opaca*)

Range
Eastern United States

Habitat
Moist woods and near the coast in sandy soil

Appearance
A small tree, growing up to 40 ft. (12 m) high, with smooth gray bark; dark green, oval-shaped leaves with prickles at the edges; the leaves stay green all year round; red, spherical berries, around ⅜ in. (1 cm) across; small white flowers between the angles of the leaves and the stem

Life cycle
Perennial

Uses
Ornamental; seasonal decorations; engraving

Status
Not evaluated

Honeyguide

Honeyguides are small, dull-colored birds that live in the remotest parts of Africa, southern Asia, and Malaysia. They live in forests and open woodlands and are never far from colonies of bees.

GUIDING CALL

Insects form the major part of the diet of most small birds, but the honeyguide is unique. In addition to eating the grubs of bees, it eats the wax comb of beehives. It is the behavior of the greater honeyguide (*Indicator indicator*) that explains how this group of birds got its name. Wild African bees build their nests in hollow trees or clefts in rocks. The greater honeyguide cannot get into the hive by itself, because its bill is slender and delicate. When a honeyguide spots a bees' hive, it goes off in search of someone who can open it up. It attracts the attention of a honey badger or a human (both are great honey lovers) with a persistent, chattering call. When the honeyguide has caught their attention, it flies in short bursts toward the bees' hive, checking to see that it is being followed.

Once it reaches the hive, the honeyguide sits patiently and waits while the human or

▼ *Perched on a honeycomb in the decayed tree trunk that a swarm of bees chose for its hive, this greater honeyguide is enjoying a feast.*

honey badger takes down the hive to get at the honey. The honey badger eats what it wants of the honey and leaves the indigestible honeycomb for the bird. However, a human "helper" usually takes the comb away to drain it and eat it. Among the local African people, tradition demands that a person should leave the bird at least part of the honeycomb, spiked on a twig or put in some other prominent place. How the honeyguide learned to find a helper, and how the people and honey badgers learned to follow, is a mystery. The scaly-throated honeyguide (*Indicator variegatus*) behaves like the greater honeyguide in calling helpers to a hive.

REPRODUCTIVE HELPERS

When honey is around, the honeyguide seems a friendly little bird. However, at breeding time its behavior toward other birds is not so friendly. Like the North American cowbird and the European cuckoo, the honeyguide is lazy about nesting. It never builds its own nest,

but lays its eggs in the nests of other birds. It selects a host that nests in banks and holes in trees, such as a bee-eater, kingfisher, or woodpecker, and lays one or two eggs. The female may puncture the eggs of the host species to prevent them from developing.

When it hatches, the honeyguide throws the host bird's young out of the nest or attacks them with a sharp hook on the tip of its beak. The host bird then has to rear the young honeyguide until it is ready to fly off alone. It is thought that all 17 species of honeyguides breed in this way.

It has been shown in laboratory tests that young honeyguides eat bee grubs and wax from a very early age, without ever being taught by an adult bird. Scientists have not been able to find any reason why these particular grubs and the wax are such an important part of the diet. The young honeyguides, once they have left the nest, develop the characteristic call that attracts humans or honey badgers to beehives without ever hearing it from their parents.

▲ *Other species of honeyguides, including the lesser honeyguide (Indicator minor), shown here, also eat wax, grubs, and honey from the comb, but they do not guide mammals to the site to help them get at the hive.*

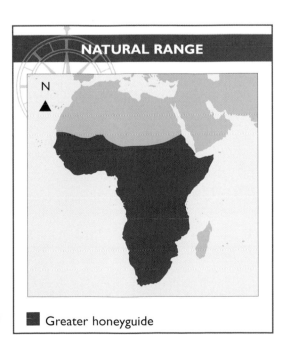

NATURAL RANGE

N

■ Greater honeyguide

See also **Badger, Bee-eater, Birds, Cuckoo, Perching birds, Woodpecker**

HOOFED MAMMALS

Hoofed mammals, or ungulates, are mammals that have replaced their claws with hooves during the course of evolution. A hoof is a tough covering that encases toes and protects them from wear and tear. It is made of keratin, the same substance that forms hair and nails.

Almost all ungulates are large land-living mammals that graze or browse plants. The 244 species alive today fall into two groups. Even-toed ungulates, the artiodactyls, have two or four toes. The perissodactyls, or odd-toed ungulates, have one or three functional toes. Paenungulates (formerly subungulates) are another group that share anatomical characteristics. The members of this last group are elephants, hyraxes, and the aardvark.

WHY HOOVES?

Hooves are a feature that help most ungulates run far and fast to escape large, swift predators. Ungulates walk or run on the tips of their toes with the heel raised off the ground. By swinging each leg in a wide forward and backward arc beneath the body, most ungulates can cover a lot of ground in a single stride. The hoof-protected toes help transmit the animal's weight through just a few strong upright bones.

GRAZERS

Although ungulates vary greatly in size, from deer less than 3 feet (0.9 m) tall to massive, barrel-bodied hippopotamuses and rhinoceroses, they have many features in common. As grazers or browsers of plants, many special features help ungulates gather and digest stems and leaves. Unable to use their feet to grasp and pluck plant material, ungulates have long tongues and mobile lips to do the job. Their front teeth (incisors) break off leaves and stems, while their cheek teeth (premolars and molars) have large, ridged surfaces that grind the plant material into a pulp before swallowing. To help pulverize the food, the lower jaw moves from side to side against the upper jaw. The gut is long and complex, because fiber-rich plant food is difficult to digest. To gain enough energy and nutrients from their food, many ungulates spend much of their waking lives eating. Ruminant ungulates chew their food twice.

UNGULATE SENSES

Ungulates are favorite prey of large land predators such as big cats and members of the dog family, including wolves. Most ungulates have well-developed senses of sight, sound, and smell. These give early warning of danger, so the animal can flee in good time. Ungulates can rotate their ears in the direction of sound. Their eyes are large and placed on the side of the head, so they give a wide field of view.

EVEN-TOED UNGULATES

The artiodactyls, or even-toed ungulates, are the most varied and widespread group of large land mammals alive today, with some 225 species. Their natural range

◄ *Primitive mammals initially had five toes on each foot. When the first horses evolved, they had three toes. In the modern horse, only the middle "third" toe remains.*

▲ *There are many species of even-toed ungulates, such as pigs, which have four toes and belong to the family Suidae. Pigs are examples of artiodactyls. Pigs are strong, intelligent creatures that adapt well to different environments.*

includes all continents except Australasia and Antarctica. Artiodactyls include familiar farm animals, such as pigs, cows, and sheep, and wild deer, cattle, bison, and antelope. Artiodactyls shape many landscapes through their browsing on trees or grazing on grasses. They have either two or four weight-bearing toes on each foot. The weight-bearing toes, with a gap between third and fourth toes, forms a split or cloven hoof.

Most artiodactyls bear permanent horns or seasonal antlers on the crown of the head, especially in males. These structures may be used for defense. In males they serve as an advertisement to potential mates and can be used in ritual battles between males to claim a female.

Most artiodactyls are ruminants. This means they have a chamber in the stomach, called the rumen, which receives freshly swallowed plant food. The food ferments in this chamber through the action of helpful bacteria (single-celled organisms). The bacteria help digest the tough, fibrous material that makes up the walls of plant cells. After many hours in the rumen, the partially digested food, called cud, is regurgitated (returned to the mouth). The animal then chews the cud before swallowing it. This time the food bypasses the rumen and travels through three stomach chambers before entering the rest of the digestive system. This "double digestion" can take several days and helps extract the maximum amount of energy and nutrients from plant food.

ODD-TOED UNGULATES

Among odd-toed ungulates, horses, asses, and zebras bear their weight on a single, very long middle ('third') toe. The other toes are completely missing, fused, or small and nonfunctional. In rhinoceroses and tapirs, the three middle toes bear the weight and the outer two are redundant or missing. Tapirs are unusual in that they have four functional toes on their front feet. Of all perissodactyls, only rhinoceroses grow horns.

Unlike ruminant artiodactyls, perissodactyls do not have a massively enlarged stomach with several chambers. Instead, the fermenting bacteria live in an outer fold of the gut, the cecum, and in the hindgut, not in the stomach. Perissodactyls do not chew the cud and so do not digest plant matter as efficiently as ruminant artiodactyls.

CONNECTIONS

Compare
The complex digestive system of hoofed mammals, which eat plant material, to that of CARNIVORES, which have a simple digestive system to accommodate animal prey.

Find out more about
Some particular hoofed mammals in these articles:

- BUFFALO
- CAMEL
- DEER
- ELAND
- ELEPHANT
- GOAT
- HIPPOPOTAMUS
- IBEX
- LLAMA
- RHINOCEROS
- TAPIR
- ZEBRA

Hornbill

As their name implies, hornbills are famous for their horn-shaped bills, which often have serrated (sawlike) edges for cutting up food. Most species live in lush forests in Africa and Asia, but some of the African species live in drier savanna habitats.

BIG BEAKS

In many species of hornbills, the large bill is crowned by a casque. This helmetlike structure may be a narrow, bony ridge that reinforces the upper bill. However, in some species it is much more elaborate, a sort of tube that may be larger than the bill itself. This gives the bill a very heavy look, but it is actually extremely light.

Both males and females have casques, but they are usually larger and more elaborate in the males. Scientists are not quite sure about the purpose of the casque. In the great and rhinoceros hornbills, it is used in fighting or to knock down fruit. It

KEY FACTS

Name

Red-billed hornbill (*Tockus erythrorhynchus*)

Range

Africa, south of the Sahara

Habitat

Scrub and open woodlands

Appearance

20 in. (50 cm); mainly white or gray, with black markings on the wings and tail; strong downwardly curved red bill

Food

Insects and fruit

Breeding

Nest hole usually 45–90 ft. (15–30 m) above ground in a tall forest tree; the female shuts herself in and incubates the eggs for 30–45 days; the male feeds the female and the young

Status

Least concern

◄ *The red-billed hornbill of Africa has a characteristic downward-curving bill.*

500

may be used in recognizing the age, sex, and species of an individual. It also might amplify the hornbill's song.

Hornbills are particularly noisy birds, giving high-pitched cries and whistles, usually with their heads raised so that their bills point upward. One species makes ever louder and faster hoots until it breaks into a maniacal laugh—a characteristic sound of the Asian rain forests. Hornbills also make loud whirring noises as they flap their wings in flight. They are usually seen in pairs or in small groups, though larger numbers may congregate at a tree when the fruit is ripe. Some species live on the ground. Other hornbills sleep in roosts in tall trees for much of the year; as many as 100 have been counted at a single roost.

SEALED NESTS

The nesting habits of the majority of hornbills are unique. The pair selects a suitable hole in a hollow tree, or sometimes a cavelike crevice in rock. After mating, the female seals herself into the hole, using material supplied

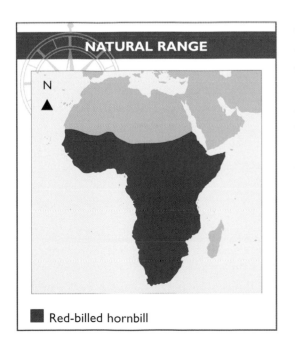

NATURAL RANGE

N

■ Red-billed hornbill

▲ *This rhinoceros hornbill shows off his huge casque (the top part of his bill). His mate and young are sealed into a nest in the hollow of a tree, and he is supplying them with food. He will take away food remains and droppings to keep the nest clean.*

by the male (usually earth mixed with sticky mucus). She pats this into the entrance hole until she is sealed in, with only a narrow slit left open. The male brings food to the nest and passes it to the female (and later to the nestlings). In some species the male continues to feed the female and her young until the young are ready to leave the nest. In other species the female breaks out when the chicks are about half grown and helps with the work of feeding them. The chicks then reseal the nest and break out only when they are ready to fly. This habit protects the young from predators.

See also **Birds, Perching birds, Toucan**

Hornet

Hornets are generally thought of as insects to be avoided, because the sting of these large wasps is very painful. Because they are large, and make loud buzzing noises, hornets are often perceived to be dangerous. However, they are more likely to sting if people swat at them. If a hornet is buzzing around, it is better to avoid it. When a hornets' nest is disturbed, hundreds of worker hornets will defend the nest and sting anyone nearby.

Although a single sting from a hornet is not usually a problem, multiple stings may cause severe reactions. These wasps are responsible for several deaths each year in

▲ *The hornet, like other members of the wasp family, has a distinctive narrow waist between the thorax and the abdomen, which gives rise to the description "wasp-waisted" for someone with a very slim waistline.*

the United States. Occasionally, people have a serious allergic reaction to hornet stings, and this reaction can be fatal if the right drugs are not given very quickly.

NESTS OF PAPER

Hornets are part of the family Vespidae. All the wasps in this family live in large social groups and are able to make a type of paper to construct their delicate nests. Favorite sites for hornets' nests are under the eaves of buildings or in trees. As long as they are left alone, the hornets keep busy building the nest and feeding their grubs, but if they are disturbed, they become very aggressive. In the swamps of Florida, they often build their nests on branches that hang down over the water. As the swamps were opened up for tourism, many explorers found themselves crashing into the nests before they even noticed them.

Hornets build a new nest each year. The process starts in the spring, when queen hornets come out of hibernation. A queen hornet finds a site and then starts to build a nest. She uses plant material and wood from trees and fences. First she scrapes away some of the material, and then she mashes it up with her mandibles (jaws), moistening it with saliva. She builds a small papery bell, open at the lower end, and in the middle she makes a layer of cells. To start with there are only a few cells, which the queen fills with eggs. When they hatch, she has to feed them.

After a month, the grubs have grown so large that they fill their cells. They seal themselves in and pupate. A week later, the first grubs emerge as adults. The first to emerge are always workers, which are female. They help feed the next batch of larvae and continue to build the nest until there are several layers of cells encased in an outer covering of paper. In some species the whole structure takes on the shape of a football. At this point the queen can devote all her time to laying eggs. As the workers emerge, the queen goes back and refills each cell.

SPECIAL DIET

Adult hornets feed on carbohydrates, which are sweet and sugary foods from flowers and fruit. This gives them the energy they need to travel long distances in search of food. The grubs need a high-protein diet for rapid growth, so they are fed on insects. Toward the end of the summer, some of the cells are fed on slightly different diets to create new queens, and some unfertilized eggs become male hornets. In the fall, the new queens and males emerge and fly together to mate. The queens are fertilized and then hibernate. Workers are killed by the first frosts. In the spring the whole process starts again.

See also **Bee, Invertebrates, Wasp**

KEY FACTS

Name
Hornet (*Vespa* and *Vespula* species)

Range
All continents except Antarctica

Habitat
Temperate and subtropical woodlands, gardens, and outbuildings

Appearance
Up to 1½ in. (4 cm) long; brown and yellow bands around the abdomen; the wings folded when at rest

Food
Adults eat fruit and nectar; the larvae are fed on insects

Breeding
Queen fertilized in the fall and carries sperm through hibernation; she builds the nest and lays eggs in the spring

Status
Not evaluated

◀ *The hornets' cells are hexagonal (six-sided) tubes that fit together with no gaps between. The white coverings are created when the grubs are pupating.*

Horse

In the Wild West, herds of wild horses roamed over much of the American plains. There is now no such thing as a wild horse. All populations of modern-day "wild" horses came about as a result of domestic horses escaping or being released back into the wild. In fact, when Europeans first arrived in

▼ These mustangs, living wild on the Western plains, are descended from horses that were brought to America by Spanish settlers 400 years ago.

the New World in the fifteenth century, there were no horses at all in either North or South America. Spanish colonizers brought the species to America in the late 1500s.

However, fossils show that horses or their relatives once did exist in North America. They seem to have disappeared from the North American plains 8,000 years ago, soon after humans came to the continent. Sixty million years earlier, a small five-toed creature the size of a large dog lived in the North American forests. This animal, the *Hyracotherium,* was probably the first horse species. Fossils of horses of various shapes and sizes have been found. About five million years ago, there were eight or ten species of horses in North America alone, and the family had spread throughout Asia and into Africa.

SMALL ANCESTORS

Early horses were small, slow, short-legged creatures with three or five soft-padded toes formed into rudimentary hoofs. They lived in the forests where they found a variety of fruit, nuts, leaves, and other plant material to eat. As time went by, horses got larger and faster. Gradually, they began to lose some of the toes on their front and hind feet, placing most of their weight on the central toe. Their diet shifted from feeding on bushes to grazing on newly evolved grasses. Consequently, their teeth became adapted to chewing much coarser grass.

The modern horse is large and capable of fast movement. Its foot has evolved into a single, hard hoof that, with its long legs, allows it to run rapidly across the grasslands to

▶ *These feral horses live in the Carmargue in France.*

KEY FACTS
Name
Domestic horse (*Equus caballus*)
Range
North and South America, Australia
Habitat
Open plains, open woodlands, wherever grass is plentiful
Appearance
Males and females are approximately the same size, measuring up to 6½ ft. (2 m) from head to rump, and weighing up to 1,100 lb. (500 kg) in most species; enormous color variation, with gray, brown, and black being the most common colors
Food
Mainly grasses, herbs, and reeds, but will also eat tender young leaves
Breeding
Females usually give birth in the spring, 11 months after mating
Status
Not evaluated

escape from predators. All six species of modern horses, zebras, and asses are really very similar to one another. Scientists put them all in the same group, *Equus,* which implies that they share a common ancestor —probably a plains-living horse that lived about two million years ago.

USEFUL TO HUMANS

Horses were domesticated in Mongolia about 5,000 years ago. Ever since then they have been extremely important to humans. They have been used for tasks such as pulling plows and carts. Swift-footed horses provided people with the only fast form of land transportation until the invention of trains and cars. Horses also provide meat and leather. In some areas they even supply their owners with milk. Indeed, the horse is among the most adaptable of all the animals that humans have domesticated.

Since horses were domesticated, a wide variety of breeds have been developed. Professional breeders look for particular characteristics such as speed and gracefulness in the case of racehorses, or strength and power in the case of large farm horses. Many different kinds of ponies have been bred, too.

Ponies are generally smaller and stockier than other horses, with thicker coats and longer manes. Some tiny ponies, such as Dartmoor ponies, were crossbred with even smaller Shetland ponies to be small enough to work in coal mines. The smallest horse in the world is the Falabella horse from Argentina. It grows to about 3 feet (90 cm).

RETURN TO THE WILD

Horses that were once domesticated and released or escaped into the wild are called feral. Horses have been set free to roam the wild in many places, and feral horses

can be found in the Caribbean, in the deserts of the southwestern United States, the high-altitude plains of the Rocky Mountains, the deserts of Australia, and the pampas (temperate grasslands) of South America.

One of the things that makes horses so adaptable is their diet. Unlike cows and antelope, which need fine, green grass to survive, horses are able to eat many kinds of grass, even the coarse, dry variety. They are also able to process food much more quickly than bovids (cows and cowlike animals). When only poor-quality food is available, bovids die because they can't digest it, while horses thrive by eating more and pushing the food faster through their digestive system.

SOCIAL BEASTS

Most of what is known about the social behavior of wild horses is taken from scientists' observations of feral horses, such as Przewalski's horse, which has been bred in captivity and released into the wild again.

Horses live in family groups called harems, which are made up of one male and usually up to five females. Each of these harems has its own home range and is a tight and stable family unit. Harems never split up, moving

▲ *During the nineteenth century, the only truly wild horse was found on the Mongolian plains of Central Asia. It was originally "discovered" by a Polish explorer named Nikolai Przewalski and has since been called Przewalski's horse (shown above). Soon after their discovery, Przewalski's horses became extinct in the wild. Only now, after decades of captive breeding, are Przewalski's horses being brought back to Mongolia to roam wild again.*

from their winter territories to their summer grazing areas as one unit.

In most parts of the world, horses are very seasonal breeders, and the young are born soon after the spring begins. Horses are able to breed again almost immediately after giving birth. A female horse (mare) will only mate with the male (stallion) in her family group. Because horses have an 11-month gestation period (the time when the baby is growing inside its mother), the young are born at about the same time every year.

LEAVING THE FAMILY GROUP

Young horses (foals) stay in their family group for a fairly long period of time compared to many other animals. Males leave their family group when they are 18 to 24 months old and join up with other young nonbreeding males (colts) in bachelor groups.

The membership of bachelor groups is extremely stable; the young males leave the group only when they are old enough to start their own harem, or to fight a stallion for control of an existing one.

Young females (fillies) leave their family groups when they are 16 to 18 months old.

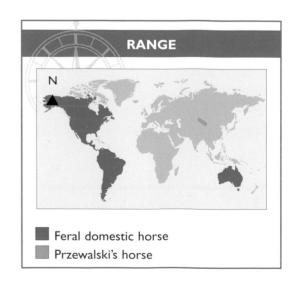

RANGE

■ Feral domestic horse
■ Przewalski's horse

KEY FACTS

Name

Przewalski's horse
(*Equus przewalskii*)

Range

Central Mongolia

Habitat

Grasslands and high-
altitude semideserts

Appearance

A sturdy horse,
measuring up to 7 ft.
(2.1 m) from head to
rump, and weighing
800 lb. (350 kg);
dun-colored flanks
and yellowish white
underparts; the mane
is stiff and erect and
a deep, dark brown;
a large head, and
short, dark legs

Food

Mainly grasses

Breeding

Similar to the
domestic horse

Status

Not evaluated

At this time they are ready to breed and produce their own foals. Fillies will frequently join an existing harem, but they never stay in the harem in which they were born. By doing this, horses avoid inbreeding. Females will sometimes change groups if they think another male will better protect them and their foals.

Scientists who study the domestication of wild animals often wonder why some animals tame very easily and others can never be domesticated. One thing that may make horses so easy to domesticate is the way they organize their social life. All horses leave the family group in which they are born, so they are used to being moved out of a social group. Yet all horses join new groups and are very loyal to the members of this group even though they are not closely related. This loyalty to the group may explain why horses are so loyal to their owners.

FOREST HORSES OF EUROPE

Until the Late Middle Ages, approximately 800 years ago, a rare horse called the tarpan lived in European forests. Scientists believe that the extinction of the tarpan may have been caused by humans. The forests were cut down to make way for farmland, and the horses were probably killed for their meat and hides.

Very little is known about the tarpan, except that it existed in Europe for thousands of years. Tarpans or other wild horses are commonly found in the cave paintings of southern France and were used by early humans as a source of food. Scientists think that tarpans may have been the same species as either Przewalski's or domestic horses, but they may never know for sure.

See also **Hoofed mammals, Mammals,
Wild ass, Zebra**

▶ *Although she will
be weaned at about
13 months, this foal
will stay with her
mother until she is
16–18 months old.
Then she will be
ready to leave her
family group.*

Horse chestnut

Horse chestnuts and their relatives make up a small family of trees and shrubs that are native mainly to North America and Asia. Most species have eye-catching clusters of flowers in spring and summer, so they are often grown as ornamental plants. North American members of the horse chestnut family are called buckeyes. They include the Ohio buckeye, the state tree of Ohio.

The horse chestnut tree itself is a European species, native to the mountains of Greece and Albania but now widely planted elsewhere. Despite its name, it is not related to the true or sweet chestnut, which belongs to a different family, although both trees produce similar-looking large brown seeds. The seeds of horse chestnuts and buckeyes contain poisonous chemicals.

SIZE AND HABITS

Except for two tropical species, all members of the horse chestnut family are classified within a single genus, *Aesculus*. The largest tree in the whole family is the yellow buckeye, *Aesculus flava,* which can reach a height of 100 feet (30 m). It is found in forests of the east-central United States. The common or European horse chestnut (*Aesculus hippocastanum*), which is often grown in parks, is also a large tree. The Ohio buckeye (*Aesculus glabra*) may reach 60 to 70 feet (18 to 21 m) high, but is usually smaller. The other five species of North American buckeyes are small trees or shrubs. An example is the California buckeye (*Aesculus californica*), which is adapted to survive in dry regions.

▲ *The horse chestnut is a deciduous tree (it loses its leaves in winter). Horse chestnut trees can be recognized by their large handlike leaves and tall spikes of pink or white flowers, which look like candles.*

The two tropical species of the horse chestnut family belong to the genus *Billia,* and are both evergreen trees. They grow in forests in the tropical Americas, especially on the slopes of mountains.

SPECIAL FEATURES

The leaves of the horse chestnut family are unusual. Each leaf is large, but divided into five to seven leaflets, like the fingers of a hand. There are slight shape differences among species. The Japanese horse chestnut, *Aesculus turbinata,* has the largest leaves, growing up to

STATE TREE
OHIO

Name
Buckeye
(*Aesculus glabra*)

Habitat
Favors rich soils,
especially near rivers

Range
From Ohio west
to Illinois and Iowa,
south to Texas,
Tennessee, Oklahoma,
and Kansas

Life cycle
Flowers April–
May; fruits ripen
in September

Status
Not evaluated

► *The Indian horse chestnut (Aesculus indica) contains substances called saponins in its seeds, which can be used as a soap substitute. The seeds also used to be given to horses to cure colic.*

2 feet (60 cm) across. In the genus *Billia*, the leaves have only three leaflets.

Like other trees and shrubs of cooler regions, *Aesculus* horse chestnuts and buckeyes lose their leaves in the fall. In winter their twigs have large resting buds, ready to produce shoots in the spring. The buds of European species of horse chestnuts are sticky. This makes them easy to tell from American buckeyes, which have nonsticky buds.

Horse chestnuts and buckeyes have colorful flowers, grouped in vertical spikes or candles. These attract insects that fertilize them by carrying pollen from one flower to another. (In contrast, conifers are pollinated by the wind, and so have no need for showy flowers.) The flower spikes of the red buckeye (*Aesculus pavia*) are scarlet, while the spike shape of another species, *Aesculus parviflora*, gives it its common name, which is bottlebrush buckeye.

After fertilization, the round, greenish fruits begin to grow. They vary between species: some are smooth, while others have spines or prickles. When they ripen and fall, usually in September, they split and release between one and three large seeds. Each seed is shiny brown, with a large white patch. The color pattern of the seeds is the origin of the name "buckeye," from its resemblance to the eye of a buck (male deer).

USES
The most widespread use of horse chestnuts and buckeyes is ornamental. An avenue of horse chestnuts in spring, covered with hundreds of flowering candles, is an impressive sight. Plant breeders have created many new colorful varieties for use in parks and gardens.

The wood of horse chestnuts is too soft and weak to be used in building. It can be made into wood pulp, and it has also been used for artificial limbs. The seeds are occasionally eaten, but they have to be specially prepared to get rid of the bitter, poisonous substances they contain.

See also **Flowering plants, Temperate forests**

Horseshoe bat

Horseshoe bats are one of the largest families of bats. Like other bats, horseshoe bats are expert nighttime fliers, which they achieve through a unique kind of "sound-imaging" sense, which is connected to the squashed appearance of the snout.

There are about 70 different species (types), living in various parts of Africa, Asia, Europe, and Australia, but they are all very similar. Like all bats, they all have forelimbs with skin stretched between extremely long finger bones, forming wings. What sets horseshoe bats apart, among many other features, is their faces. Horseshoe bats have a curved fleshy flap around their snout in the shape of a horseshoe. Inside this horseshoe is a complex arrangement of further knobs and flaps. The central one, jutting forward, is usually called a nose leaf.

Horseshoe bats have a stout, barrel-shaped body, but even the largest, Hildebrandt's horseshoe bat (*Rhinolophus hildebrandti*) of eastern Africa, weighs no more than 1¼ ounces (35 g). The legs are extremely thin and spindly and are used mostly for hanging upside down. Horseshoe bats spend more time hanging than most other bats. They tend not to crawl or support their body with their hind legs. Their wings are broad, which gives the bats very maneuverable flight, allowing them to flit deftly through undergrowth, while chasing their prey of moths and beetles. Some species, such as the greater horseshoe bat of Europe and Asia (*Rhinolophus ferrumequinum*), prefer to hunt from a perch like a flycatcher—scanning its surroundings, making a catch, then returning to its perch to eat its meal.

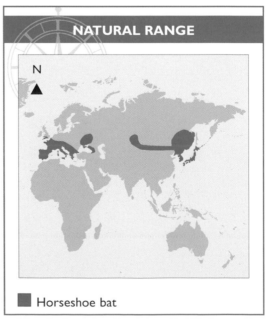

NATURAL RANGE

N

■ Horseshoe bat

▲ *Horseshoe bats have a very distinctive structure around their nose and mouth that they use to detect their prey. The curved shape of the snout helps them focus a sound in a precise direction. From the echoes they receive back through their ears, the bats can tell what types of insects are around and how close they are.*

FLYING IN THE DARK

Like nearly all bats, horseshoe bats are active by night. They have an extra sense, called echolocation, that helps them get around in the dark. The bat sends out pulses of sound many times a second. Echoes return from objects in its surroundings, and the bat's brain forms pictures from the pattern of echoes, a little like a television making pictures from electrical signals. A horseshoe bat's echolocation system is more sophisticated than that of any other bat. The first part of their sound pulses are pure tones of a precise, unchanging pitch. When these sounds meet a fluttering insect, the insect's beating wings introduce rhythmic changes in the pitch and strength of the echo. When the bat listens to these changes, it can build images that tell it the size and type of insect that made the echo. Horseshoe bat sounds quickly sweep down in pitch at the end. This gives the bat's sound images a further dimension.

Scientists think that the need for precise echolocation has given horseshoe bats the added organs on their faces. The bats emit their sounds through their nostrils, and the horseshoe and noseleaf focus the sound into a forward-pointing beam.

All bats use high-pitched sound called ultrasound, which is too high for humans to hear. Most insects cannot hear ultrasound either, but some bat prey, such as many moths, have ears, which allow them to hear most bats coming in time to dive for cover. Horseshoe bats, however, use sounds so high that even moths cannot hear them.

ROOSTING

In summer, female horseshoe bats roost in groups called colonies in any large cavity, from caves and hollow trees to people's attics. They hang freely, each swinging by the feet, not crouching, clinging, or clustered like many other bats. In these colonies, the mothers raise their pups, feeding them milk. The males roost separately in smaller groups.

In winter, horseshoe bats must hibernate, because the flying insects that they eat are not active. To survive, the bats find cool caves and allow their body temperature to drop to just a few degrees above freezing. They use very little energy this way. Greater horseshoe bats hibernate hanging from the cave roof, wrapped in their wings with only their snout poking out. They warm up and become active a few times each winter, perhaps to mate. It is the pattern of mating that interests conservationists. Some species are endangered, and their populations are made up of only a handful of colonies. If scientists can discover which groups of bats mate with others, they will learn how the genes are mixed between the colonies. This mixing may be the key to the survival of the dwindling population.

See also **Bats, Fishing bat, Mammals**

KEY FACTS

Name
Greater horseshoe bat (*Rhinolophus ferrumequinum*)

Range
Across cool parts of Europe and Asia from Great Britain to Japan

Food
Moths, beetles, crane flies, other insects

Breeding
Mating mainly in fall, sometimes in winter and spring; female delays fertilization and bears a single pup in spring

Appearance
Broad wings, stout body, spindly legs, funnel-shaped ears, elaborate structures on the face, including a horseshoe and a nose leaf

Status
Near threatened

◄ *The legs of horseshoe bats are not very strong, but their claws can grip surfaces tightly, enabling them to hang upside down from cave roofs or tree branches.*

Index